Sow What?!

Sow What?!

Joy Yeager

Essence
PUBLISHING

Belleville, Ontario, Canada

Sow What?!

All Scripture quotations, unless otherwise specified, are from the *King James Version* of the Bible

ISBN: 1-894169-72-7

Essence Publishing is a Christian Book Publisher dedicated to further-ing the work of Christ through the written word. For more information, contact: 44 Moira Street West, Belleville, Ontario, Canada K8P 1S3. Phone: 1-800-238-6376. Fax: (613) 962-3055.
Email: info@essence.on.ca
Internet: www.essence.on.ca

Printed in Canada
by

Essence
PUBLISHING

Dedication

To my wonderful Lord and Savior for his matchless grace and keeping power.

To my God-fearing mother who taught me a good dose of the fear of the Lord.

To my caring father who will do for others before himself.

To my upright husband who is a wonderful family man and holds high his moral standards.

To my three children, Brandon, Amber and Amanda, whom I raise in the fear of the Lord, training them to keep their treasures in heavenly places with Christ Jesus.

To all those steadfast in the faith who have had a spiritual influence in my life.

Table of Contents

Acknowledgements

I wish to acknowledge that all parts of this book and its timing were divinely given to me by the inspiration and instruction of the Holy Spirit, from the title of the book and the chapter headings to the thoughts and many Scriptures, written under the anointing of the Lord.

I wish to express deep gratitude to my husband, Frank, for his support and advice throughout many aspects of this book. Frank, meaning honesty, certainly lives up to the meaning of his name, being a very easy-going, candid man of God.

A big hug and kiss to Brandon, who shared his room during countless hours of computer typing. Brandon, meaning a lighthouse, shared some of that light at just 14 years of age during a missions trip to El Salvador.

A special acknowledgement to Amber, my middle-schooler for her added art work. Amber, meaning precious jewel, certainly lives up to the meaning of her name.

Lots of love to Amanda for allowing Mom the quiet time necessary while seeking the Lord for instruction and direction. Amanda, who was our special needs baby, has a very fitting name, meaning worthy of love.

Thank you Pastor Roger Cales for your words of exhortation added to the back cover. Roger, meaning mighty warrior, has not only proven to be a strong church leader, but also a mighty warrior for the Lord.

Introduction

*I*t was April 29, 1998, while I was standing in front of the bathroom mirror getting ready for Wednesday evening Bible study, when the Lord spoke very vividly to me. He asked me the question that I ask my readers in the 11th chapter: "Is there such a thing as just enough heaven to keep you out of hell?" I responded, "But Lord, that's a sermon. I am not a preacher." The answer came back plain as day: "No, but you are a writer; it's time to get started."

Two days later, after I had tentatively forgot all about this experience, while I was sitting in my first Benny Hinn Crusade, the Lord spoke very vividly again, and the anointing just came pouring in. He revealed to me several of the chapter headings and what the basic design of the book should be. He gave me the dates that He wanted me to have certain aspects of the manuscript and publication completed by, and things did move accordingly.

The following months only brought about one confirmation after another that my vision was truly God sent and He had gone before me and ordered my steps. God has been magnificent in my life. I can't offer Him enough thanks for all that He's done for me.

I reflect throughout my book on the great insights I learned through personal struggles. The Lord has taken me through many years of continual battles to develop in me the character needed for the ministry He was preparing me for. I sensed for a long time that He was preparing me for something awesome, but life's troubles kept pouring my way.

Blessed be the name of the Lord! I am a living testimony that the greater the battle, the greater the victory! He has closed many doors in my life, only to open up the windows of glory!

First, let's begin in chapter one by studying the sowing and reaping principle. We will learn the art of discernment, identifying the difference in these Last Days between the believer, the nonbeliever and the so-called Christian by simply learning to do as the Scriptures tell us to do and "test the fruits." This is a critical issue as the coming of the Lord draweth nigh.

"For the word of God is quick, and powerful, and sharper than any two-edged sword, piercing even to the dividing asunder of soul and spirit, and of the joints and marrow, and is a *discerner* of the thoughts and intents of the heart" (Hebrews 4:12).

I go on to remind my readers of the need to be so rooted and planted in Him that when we hear the sound of the trumpet, we'll go out without a doubt. He is coming for a church without spot or wrinkle. In the fourth chapter, I share my personal testimony of how the Lord kept me in His saving grace from a very young age. We'll discover that achievement of this comes only through the fear of the Lord and His precious blood and grace that are sufficient to carry us through if we love him with all of our heart, soul and mind.

We will also search our lives and hearts to see how we are spending our valuable time on this earth. Over and over, I urge my readers to set their affection in the heavenlies, laying their earthly treasures at His feet. It is crucial that we keep our treasures in things above and stay rooted until the end.

Chapter six goes into a detailed description of specific sins that Christians tend to be more vulnerable to. We could never be so naive as to think we could never fall into sin, but certain sins are more subtle than some of the more obvious sins to someone with roots in the Church.

In chapter seven I remind my readers of the dangers of falling into the trap of becoming judgmental. We will explore many areas in our lives where the devil often attempts to look for an open window.

The next chapter takes an in depth look at the struggle to put off the old and put on the new, along with spiritual warfare and persecution in the Church. We will learn of the dangers of hardening our hearts toward God.

Chapter nine is dedicated to the question, "Why God?" an issue that certainly baffles a lot of people in a world of constant confusion. The following chapter challenges my readers to consider what marks they are leaving on this earth. What will you be remembered for?

The final chapter ends on a positive note reminding us that apart from the precious blood of Jesus Christ, we can do nothing. We must never think that we have "arrived." The Holy Spirit continually reminds us to stay close to the cross of Jesus Christ and keep our eyes on Him.

The twelve chapters of this book involve an intense search of the Word of God, meditating on its urge to Christians to keep themselves clean and holy before Him as signs of His appearing draw near. Many Scriptures are used not only to avoid personal perspective and opinions, but because there is no greater reference on the subject of "Holiness and the Fear of the Lord" than the Bible itself.

May God bless and keep you every moment of your life.

1

Reaping or Weeping?

"...for whatsoever a man soweth, that shall he also reap" (Galatians 6:7).

"You are what you eat." "We can't rebuke the harvest." "You made your bed, now lie in it." "He has a rude awakening coming." "What goes around, comes around." "I told you so." "Well, I could see it coming!" Painful words, but often true! The Holy Scriptures reveal this principle through Paul's writings.

"Be not deceived; God is not mocked: for whatsoever a man soweth, that shall he also reap. For he that soweth to his flesh shall of the flesh reap corruption; but he that soweth to the Spirit shall of the Spirit reap life everlasting" (Galatians 6:7-9).

Sometimes we literally pay for our mistakes the rest of our lives. Even if we receive divine forgiveness from Father God, the mistakes of our youth are often very costly. It always takes us so much longer to undo our messes than the time it takes to make them.

Take a child, for example. Turn him loose in a room for five minutes, and you'll be amazed at the amount of mess he can make in so short a time. Give him five minutes to get the room back in order – I've never met a child yet who could do it. It never ceases to amaze me how it's so much easier to walk the toys from the toy box to the floor than it is to walk the toys from the floor back to the toy box. It just doesn't seem to be possible in the same amount of time!

How true this illustration is with the messes that we get ourselves into! Is the pleasure of sin for a season, worth the price we pay for it?

Maybe it isn't the mess that we've caused. Maybe we are the victim of a problem that someone else has caused. We, then, often get upset and revengeful, only adding to the problem. To nurse a problem is to magnify it many times! How much better the results would be if we would learn to calm the storm by the silent tongue. I Thessalonians 5:15 reminds us that we are not to render evil for evil but that which is good. We are called to be peacemakers.

Fortunately, we're not only dealing with the bad things that we sow. "He which soweth sparingly shall reap also sparingly; and he which soweth bountifully shall reap also bountifully. Every man according as he purposeth in his heart, *so let him give*; not grudgingly or of necessity: For God loveth a cheerful giver" (II Corinthians 9:6,7). This is the brighter side of the coin.

There are still many good-hearted born-again Christians in the midst of an evil generation who love the Lord with all of their heart. They give of their time, energy, love and finances to help a fellow brother and for the furtherance of the kingdom of heaven. We still have people in this old world who seem to have a heart of gold, truly that of a servant. They will surely reap the fruit of their labor, and God will richly reward them for their goodness.

What Fruit Are Ye?

We live in a day and age in which we often feel we can't trust anyone. Scandals are everywhere. We can't have the assurance of safety even in our own homes. Many of the heroes in our lives have fallen to the snare of the devil. The things that go on in our nation, community, schools, churches, families and even our own homes are often downright devastating. Our lives are often wrecked by the effects of sin in our society.

How can we tell the true believers from those who turn out to be hypocrites? We all fall short at times, but some have been a *real* blow to our trust. It can take some strong spiritual discernment to decipher who's who.

I have been blessed with the gift and awesome responsibility of discernment of spirits. Few things come as a surprise to me. I have spoken many discerning, prophetic words long before they ever came to pass or were made known to the eye or ear of man. Some brought good, joyous news, but many were tragic to mankind.

Most people, however, cannot easily detect what or who to be a financial blessing to, who to trust, who to open their hurting hearts to, or know who is preparing to resign their position, change locations, or whose marriage is in trouble. We don't all have the gift of discernment, but everyone can learn to do as the Scripture instructs us and test the fruits. The closer we get to God and the more we dig into the Word, the easier it will become.

We're often told that there is a fine line between being a discerner and being judgmental, but there is a world of difference. Take a look at the definitions of the two words. To discern is "to distinguish clearly especially by the sight; to perceive by the mind; to behold as separate." The word *judge* means "to decide; to hear and try a case in a court of law; to give a final opinion or decision (as in a performance); to criticize."[1]

When we become guilty of being judgmental, we are passing sentence. As a child of God, we are not permitted to be a judge; but, as a child of God, we are qualified to be a discerner and required to use it in time of need for spiritual discernment.

"They shall teach my people *the difference* between the holy and profane, and cause them to discern between the unclean and the clean" (Ezekiel 44:23).

"For a good tree bringeth not forth corrupt fruit; neither doth a corrupt tree bring forth good fruit. For every tree is known by his own fruit. For of thorns men do not gather figs, nor of a bramble bush gather they grapes. A good man of the good treasure of his heart bringeth forth that which is good; and an evil man out of the evil treasure of his heart bringeth forth that which is evil: for of the abundance of the heart his mouth speaketh" (Luke 6:43-45).

"Beware of false prophets, which come to you in sheep's clothing, but inwardly they are ravening wolves... By their fruits, ye shall know them" (Matthew 7: 15, 20).

The following is a checklist that will aid you in the time of need for discernment:

1) Do they live the fruit of the Spirit? Love, joy, peace, long-suffering, gentleness, goodness, faith, meekness, temperance (Galatians 5:22,23).

2) Do they practice the beatitudes – meek, hungering and thirsting after righteousness, merciful, pure in heart, peacemakers at times, persecuted for righteousness' sake – as listed in Luke 6:20-26?

3) Do they show love at all costs? "Love your enemies," as in Luke 6:27-36.

4) Are they vessels of honor, sanctified, and meet for the master's use and prepared unto every good work? II Timothy 2:20-21.

5) As they journey through their Christian walk, are they learning more patience and strengthening their hearts as the coming of the Lord draweth nigh? James 5:8.

6) Do they display "wisdom from above that is pure, peaceable, gentle and easy to be entreated, full of mercy and good fruits, without partiality or hypocrisy?" James 3:17,18.

7) Do they habitually repeat negative, unedifying words, or do they keep their tongue from evil and their lips from speaking guile? Psalm 34:13.

8) How do they spend their time, their money, their hobbies? "Out of the good treasure of the heart bringeth forth good things: and an evil man out of the evil treasure bringeth forth evil things" (Matthew 12:34-37).

9) What are their motives for their good works? "Not with eye service, as men-pleasers; but as the servants of Christ, doing the will of God from the heart; with good will doing service, as to the Lord, and not to men" (Ephesians 6:6-7).

10) Are they ashamed of their former life of sin, or do they brag about it? "...What fruit had ye then in those things whereof ye are now ashamcd? For the end of those things is death" (Romans 6:20-22).

11) Do they feed their souls on the Word? "Study to show thyself approved unto God, a workman that needeth not to be ashamed, rightly dividing the word of truth" (II Timothy 2:15).

12) Do they spend quality time in prayer, intercession? "I exhort therefore, that, first of all, supplications, prayers, intercessions, and giving of thanks, be made for all men" (I Timothy 2:1).

13) Do they sing and make melody in their hearts in praise to the Lord? "Speaking to yourselves in psalms and hymns and spiritual songs, singing and making melody in your heart to the Lord; Giving thanks always for all things unto God and the Father in the name of our Lord Jesus Christ" (Ephesians 5:19,20).

14) Do they have a burden for souls? "And he saw that there was no man, and wondered that there was no intercessor" (Isaiah 59:16).

15) Are they soul winners? "Go ye therefore, and teach all nations, baptizing them in the name of the Father, and of the Son, and of the Holy Ghost" (Matthew 28:19,20).

Say What?

Last but not least, the best way to tell if a person is a true follower of Christ, is to listen carefully to what you hear coming out of their mouth. The key passage is: "Not that which goeth into the mouth defileth a man; but that which cometh out of the mouth, this defileth a man. Do not ye yet understand, that whatsoever entereth in at the mouth goeth into the belly, and is cast out into the draught? But those things which proceed out of the mouth come forth from the heart: and they defile the man. For out of the heart proceed evil thoughts, murders, adulteries, fornications, thefts, false witness, blasphemies: These are the things which defile a man" (Matthew 15: 11, 17-20).

You can tell a lot about a person by the way he talks. Have you ever met a person with an exceptionally pleasant personality and thought *Wow*, they must be a Christian? Then, you hear the way they talk and are overwhelmed with disappointment. Our tongue gives away what's on the inside!

"Let no corrupt communication proceed out of your mouth, but that which is good to the use of edifying, that it may minister grace unto the hearers. And grieve not the holy Spirit of God, whereby ye are sealed unto the day of redemption. Let all bitterness, and wrath, and anger, and clamor, and evil speaking, be put away from you, with all malice: And be ye kind one to another, tenderhearted, forgiving one another, even as God for Christ's sake hath forgiven you" (Ephesians 4:29-32).

I urge you if you are a nonbeliever, one sitting on the fence, or in the Church and wondering if it's worth it with all of the hypocrisy you've witnessed, *do not* allow the poor witness of a weak, immature or so-called Christian to keep you from eternal security. When we stand before the Lord on judgment day, we can't tell Him we never could live the Christian life because of the hypocrite down the street. That just won't cut it. As I often ask my children, "How are you going to explain that one to God?"

Notes

[1]*Webster's Dictionary*, 1989 ed.

2
And Who Are You?

"Ye are the salt of the earth..." (Matthew 5:13).

We learned in chapter one some of the ways that we can know whether other people are real Christians or not. Now let's take a look at ourselves. If we spend our time only watching other's actions, we *will* become judgmental. It is important to continuously check out our own motives and actions.

Are you a light to those around you? Do people take delight in your company? Nobody enjoys being around a grump. Are you uplifting, edifying to those who you work hand in hand with each day and to those who you fellowship with throughout the week?

Does the joy of the Lord flow out of you? Try a smile – it's contagious!

Are you the salt of the earth as we are called to be? Do you add spice to life? You know how salt adds that unbeatable flavor to the tip of your tongue. We need to make a difference in our little corner of the world.

I am not a big salt user myself. An 11 ounce container of salt lasted me about a year and a half. When I make homemade slippery pot pie, however, my taste buds change. That doughy blob just isn't edible without that added salt on the tip of my tongue. Salt makes a difference.

Are you a moon, does the Son shine through you? Is it evident that Jesus is Lord of your life? Are you a reflection of His glory? Are you like a light in the midst of darkness? Do you stand out in a crowd? In what way? Are you known for your gentle, good nature or for your harsh, cold nature?

My first grade teacher told my class on the first day of school, "There are two ways I will remember your name: if you are an extremely well-behaved student or if you are an extremely ill-behaved student. Won't you be one who I remember because you are a nice child?"

How true of the adult life. Let's face it. The television heroes are either the stars from Hollywood or the mass murderers. What impression are you leaving on those around you? Are you known for your goodness or for your violent temper? Are you known for your bar-hopping or are you known in the community for the service you do for the work of the Lord?

God is big enough that He doesn't need our help in carrying His message to others. He did enough supernatural works in just six days of creation. Even today, He displays His power in the healing of the sick and miracles. He can and does supernaturally save souls without any help from believers. He prefers, however, for us to be used as vessels of honor for getting His work done. He could do it without our help, but we are still instructed to preach and teach and bring glad tidings of the good news to every creature.

Are you wearing beautiful feet? "How beautiful are the feet of them that preach the gospel of peace, and bring glad tidings of good things!" (Romans 10:15).

Are you presenting the gospel to those you come into contact with each day? We are sermons in shoes to those we work with and live with. Do they see Jesus in you? They might not have other opportunities to hear about the Gospel of Jesus Christ. You just might be one of the few people they come into contact with who is serving the Lord.

It's easy to feel like there is not much difference between people in the Church and people in the world nowadays. There have been times when that thought has crossed my own mind. It has triggered some of the thoughts I've written throughout this book. I have, however, had the opportunity to be in the work world. I have gone out into the community and have been invited to a few weddings where the family members were not all saved, and let me assure you that there is a world of difference between the born-again and the lost. The world talks differently, and they dress differently. They feed their minds on horrible things, and they go to places different than where a rooted Christian would. Their whole disposition is totally different!

We have an awesome responsibility to do what we can to reach them. We cannot force them to accept the Lord, but sometimes the silent witness is more than anything we could ever say. Believe it or not, they are impressed by our stand for Christ. They *do* notice a difference in us.

Once, I said something that rhymed with a slang word, and someone I was working with thought they might have heard me use foul language. He stopped dead in his tracks, his mouth flew wide open, his eyes popped out and he exclaimed, "Did *you* say what I thought I heard you say?" Thank goodness I was able to assure him that I did not. I believe he would have had a heart attack if it had been the other case.

Christians *are* being watched. Down deep, the world actually respects the fact that we are so different. They would never admit it, but it is true.

Are you a golden apple in pictures of silver? Do the words that come out of your mouth lift up the broken-hearted? Do they speak peace to the storm?

My favorite Bible verse is found in Proverbs 25:11: "A word fitly spoken is like apples of gold in pictures of silver."

I've spent my life watching the positive and negative effects that the tongue has on the lives of others. Many books have been written on this subject. Many adults are scarred and tormented by the damage that an older person caused them during their childhood years because of the way they were spoken to.

A lot of mental health office schedules are booked tight with appointments for those who need counseling for the pains they carry from their past. Countless hours and millions of dollars are spent by people who just can't let go of the hurts that their parent's bitter words created.

On the brighter side, we can reflect on the times in our lives an encouraging word carried us through. Maybe you were at the end of your rope, and you felt that pat on the back with a voice that said, "You've been on my heart. I've been praying for you."

Maybe you had a difficult decision to make, and someone you looked up to came along and expressed their pride in your endeavors. Maybe a parent took the time to stop you in the hall and express gratitude for the time you spend teaching his or her child in Sunday school. It gave you the strength to go on.

We all have heard the saying, "It's not what you say, it's how you say it that counts," but personally, I have witnessed some times when what was said was way out of proportion. Things were not kept in perspective. The things that were said did not add up. They did not make sense; the facts just weren't straight. We need to be careful witnesses with our tongues.

Are you a passenger? Does God have the steering wheel in your life? Do you allow Him to choose the path that you should trod? Does He take you down the road of life? As you sit in the passenger seat, do you trust in His ability to get you there? To make the right turns? To make the gas pedal go fast enough to get you there in the proper time-frame? To hit the brake if He sees a disaster ahead?

Throughout the pages of this book you will learn of my intense struggle to let go and let God. To let Him have the control of my life. It took me many years to learn to trust in His wisdom and to surrender to His will for my life. Once I did, after a long battle, the victory was great!!

Are you an overcomer? "To him that overcometh will I grant to sit with me in my throne, even as I also overcame, and am set down with my Father in his throne" (Revelation 3:21).

We have a great big God. He forgives us at our request for all of our shortcomings. How much greater our testimony will be to those around us when we overcome our filthy habits. Those little words that we say that are not pleasing to the Heavenly Father are being picked up on by little ears in the world. They are kind of like kids – they don't miss a thing!

Many Christians have the testimony of deliverance from tobacco use at the instance of their salvation. A lot, however, do not. They have to seek the Lord's help to overcome that which is not good for their bodies. What a wonderful testimony it is to the world when a Christian overcomes that which he or she has struggled with for so long.

Bad habits are not the only things that need to be overcome as we become Saints. The Bible has a lot to say about fears, worries and anxieties. They can put a wall between ourselves and God and other people. These display a lack of trust in God's wisdom for our lives and burn a lot of our energy on negative thinking.

"There is no fear in love; but perfect love casteth out fear: because fear hath torment. He that feareth is not made perfect in love" (I John 4:18). The word *torment* is a pretty powerful word. Yet there are many lives we come into contact with everyday which are tormented by the effects of fear. It is a powerful thing; it zaps your strength – body, soul and spirit.

It has often been said that stress and fear are the cause of many of our physical ailments. There have been many studies done on the subject of how sickness and diseases are linked to stress and worries.

"Men's hearts failing them for fear, and for looking after those things which are coming on the earth: for the powers of heaven shall be shaken" (Luke 21:26). This verse could be linked to heart problems and other health problems that are caused by the anxieties we face in today's world.

The Lord does not want us to live in constant fear. He wants us to be delivered and overcome that which haunts our minds. If we are free from the cares of this life, not only will we be healthier, more wholesome people, but we will be better witnesses to those around us.

"For God hath not given us the spirit of fear; but of power, and of love, and of a sound mind" (II Timothy 1:7). He wants His people to rest in peace.

Are you a mountain mover? Do you have mustard seed faith? Do you know how to use the authority that Christ gave us in overcoming the obstacles of life?

We know the Bible tells us that if we have mustard seed faith, we can move mountains, but do we really believe it? Do we do it? Sometimes it seems that we prefer agony. We choose to go through life with the woes rather than the victory.

It's time for the Body of Christ to be weaned off of the baby bottle, grow up and get over its woes, and get on with it. We need to stop wasting valuable time, and reach the lost at all costs. They are looking for power to be displayed in our faith.

What Does God Say?

We live in a world of insecurity. We are very insecure beings. Advertisements, peers, our level of income and our level of success often lead to suggest that we are never good enough. We are constantly worried about what to wear, how to fix our hair, what to drive and how fancy or plain our houses are. We are never secure with ourselves just as we are. Society teaches us that we will never "arrive" until we have achieved all of the American dream life – something that will never happen, by the way, because we never reach a level of contentment when we strive to attain fulfillment in this life.

When we are not happy with ourselves, it not only causes us problems, but problems for those around us. Unhappiness breeds unhappiness. Misery loves company. When we are not happy, we can be sure that our neighbor isn't going to be happy either.

It is not until we learn to compare ourselves with the things of God, and not the things of this world that we will become secure and happy with ourselves. Focus on what God says about you – not what the world says about you, not what the mirror says about you, not what your bank account says about you, not what your job title suggests that you are.

If the Lord says you are righteous, then you are! If the Lord says you are holy, then you are! If the Lord says you are justified and sanctified, you are! When He heals you and delivers you from the things that have kept you in bondage for so long, stand fast therein! Do not let the priorities of this world rob you of what God wants to do in your life. Don't set your standards according to this world, but fix your mind on Jehovah.

He will strengthen you and establish you. He will build you up. Listen to what He has to say about you. He does not want you to walk in defeat, but in victory in Christ Jesus.

3

A Call to Holiness

"Be ye holy; for I am holy" (I Peter 1:16).

Recently when I was in the waiting room at the doctor's office, my daughter picked up an absolutely charming book, *Children's Letters to God*. It had numerous hilarious letters written by very young children, but one in particular just captured my heart.

Dear God,

What does it mean you are a jealous God. I thought you had everything.

Jane[1]

What this dear precious little girl doesn't realize is that God actually does not have everything. There are many hearts and lives He longs to have, but because of man's sinful nature, His heart is often grieved.

Dear Jane,

Unfortunately, God does get a bit jealous of the gods and idols that tend to take His place. You are a precious little girl after God's own heart. Be sure to keep Jesus Number One in your life.

Love and Prayers,

Joy

The Lord is calling His people in these Last Days to a very high level of holiness. Not that He ever tolerated anything less, but the time is so short that He wants His children to walk in the light so strongly that all will know that we are His disciples. He wants us to be sanctified and sold out to the cause of the Gospel. We've all heard the saying, "Christianity costs you nothing, yet it costs you everything!"

"Whosoever will come after me, let him deny himself, and take up his cross, and follow me. For whosoever will save his life shall lose it; but whosoever shall lose his life for my sake and the gospel's, the same shall save it. For what shall it profit a man, if he shall gain the whole world, and lose his own soul?" (Mark 8:34-36).

It is vitally important for our spiritual well-being that we search our souls to see if we are clean and holy before Him every day. He made it clear over and over again in the Scriptures that He is coming for a church without spot or wrinkle, holy and without blame. Taking up our cross means loving God more than people, more than our vehicles, more than our jobs. It means partaking of no parts of darkness, setting ourselves apart for the Savior and being sold out to him. It means loving God with all of our body, soul and spirit.

May we pray with the psalmist David, "Search me, O God, and know my heart: try me, and know my thoughts: and see if there be any wicked way in me, and lead me in the way everlasting" (Psalm 139:23,24). What a beautiful prayer, one that God will certainly honor if we pray it with sincerity.

Straight Street

"Enter ye in at the strait gate: for wide is the gate, and broad is the way, that leadeth to destruction, and many there be which go in thereat: Because strait is the gate, and narrow is the way, which leadeth unto life, and few there be that find it" (Matthew 7:13,14).

The road to eternity in heaven requires no turning to the left, no turning to the right, no bends or twists. Tunnel vision only, always keeping our eyes on Jesus. Remember what happened to Peter when he took his eyes off of Jesus? He began to sink! Our Christian walk does not allow for righteous living one day and a spiritual vacation the next.

Now, we are emotional beings. Don't ever believe the myth that we will be on top of things emotionally all of the time. If we study the lives of the great heroes of the Bible, we quickly see that Paul, Peter, David and Job were often emotional yo-yos. Spiritually, however, we need to stay rooted. It's not an on/off journey. We need to keep on track and not wander off the path. We will find that when we are strengthened spiritually, our emotions will usually come in order.

It is so much harder once we've known Christ, to come back to Him if we regress to our old sinful ways. "For if after they have escaped the pollutions of the world through the knowledge of the Lord and Savior Jesus Christ, they are again entangled therein, and overcome, the latter end is worse with them than the beginning. For it had been better for them not to have known the way of righteousness, than, after they have known it, to turn from the holy commandment delivered unto them" (II Peter 2:20,21).

All of my life I've had a burning burden for souls, but it's been especially heavy for those who are riding the fence – one foot in the Church, the other in the world, those who are lukewarm, those who once were very active in the Church but have sort of taken a vacation.

Maybe they are caught up in their career for a season or just not taking life too serious for the time being. Worse, yet, maybe they have been in the Church all of their lives, serve faithfully in their positions week after week, service after service, but serve the work of the Lord instead of the Lord of the work. Some of them are as hell-bound as the prostitute off of the street who is living in continuous sin. It is a straight and narrow path. Heed to the Word of the Lord, dear friend. "For many are called but few chosen" (Matthew 6:16). "If the righteous scarcely be saved, where shall the ungodly and sinner appear? (I Peter 4:18). My heart grieves for lost souls.

Woe to the lukewarm on judgment day! They go through life thinking that God will tolerate their stagnant ways. They have been blinded to the truth. "Having a form of godliness, but denying the power thereof: from such turn away" (II Timothy 3:5). "Ever learning, and never able to come to the knowledge of the truth" (II Timothy 3:7). "They profess that they know God; but in works they deny him, being abominable, and disobedient, and unto every good work reprobate" (Titus 1:16).

It's so difficult to comprehend the shock that this type of person will experience when he/she stands before God. They went through life thinking that survival was good enough, never getting too serious with God, but never getting too involved with the world's evil

either. They think God's somehow just magically over-
looked the fact that they sometimes didn't have all of
their priorities quite straight. "Not every one that saith
unto me, Lord, Lord, shall enter into the kingdom of
heaven; but he that doeth the will of my Father which
is in heaven. Many will say to me in that day, Lord,
Lord, have we not prophesied in thy name? And in thy
name have cast out devils? And in thy name done many
wonderful works? And then will I profess unto them, I
never knew you: depart from me, ye that work iniquity"
(Matthew 7:21-23). Wow, talk about a rude awakening!

Get the picture. A middle-aged lady is suddenly
killed in a tragic car accident. News of this tragedy
leaves the community in shock as she was a much loved
person. Many people assumed she found her resting
place in heaven. However, she is eternally tormented as
she hears the horrifying words, "I never knew you. You
did all those good works unto yourself, in your own
name. Your motive was not holy, it was not done in service to the Lord."

In shock, she squeals, "But God, I served my community in great ways, served on the school PTA, fed the
poor, volunteered at the hospitals. How could this be?"
Then the Lord replies, "I never knew you. Depart ye
worker of iniquity."

Shakening

My, how we need to keep our guard and stay rooted!
We are living in such a time that it's crucial that we are
planted in Him, immovable. All that can be shaken, will
be shaken! "Let no man deceive you by any means: For
that day shall not come, except there come a falling

away first, and that man of sin be revealed, the son of
perdition" (II Thessalonians 2:3).

It's hard to imagine the trauma of those who are left
behind when the rapture takes place. Get the picture –
two friends will be talking on the phone, one saved, the
other not. All of a sudden, one will realize she's talking
to herself. Some will experience the trauma of the person standing next to them disappearing before their
very eyes. Neighbors will wonder, *where did those holy
rollers go on vacation to this week? Are they in a week
long revival again?* Homes and businesses will be broken into more than ever before as it is realized that the
building is now unoccupied. Loan officers will go crazy,
wondering how they will ever retrieve all those loan
payments. Babies will be reported missing. Cars will
crash. Airplanes will lose their pilots. Employers will be
writing up pink slips for all those who didn't bother to
call in. *Where is he today? His attendance has always
been perfect! Was he in an accident? What will we do, no
one ever cross-trained for his position!*

Many will be in shock when they come to realize
that all those missing were born-again Christians! Well,
they knew about the Lord, attended a few services at
the local church, lived a relatively good life, meant to
give God their all some day.... But it's a day too late.
"Behold, I come quickly" (Revelation 22:12).

Seem unfair? Even the strongest of Christians often
have that thought, *God just isn't fair.* I certainly have.
I've often wondered why God didn't create Heaven, hell
and la-de-da-da land ...you know the land about 2000
feet above the ground that is created for the lukewarm
Christian, the one that's not bad enough for hell, nor

sold out enough for heaven.

God has shown enough of His goodness that we have no excuse to offer Him. He has placed us in a country where we have freedom of religion. Our opportunities to grow in the Lord are immense in America. There are so many modern technologies available via Bibles, books, tapes, television, radio, preachers, evangelists. Our resources are endless! It's not hard to find a good Bible-believing church or make solid Christian friendships. We are so blessed!

Whether we feel that life is fair or not, it still does not change the facts. There are only two choices; there is heaven and there is hell. There is no middle ground, no la-de-da-da land. Christ is coming for a bride without spot or wrinkle. The bottom line is, we need to be ready whether we like it or not.

Free to Fear

How do you begin to live a holy life? Through a good dose of the fear of the Lord! "And I will make an ever-lasting covenant with them, that I will not turn away from them, to do them good; but I will put my fear in their hearts, that they shall not depart from me" (Jeremiah 32:40).

We'll often hear someone say, "I love the Lord with all of my being," yet, they obviously neglect to delight in the fear of the Lord. When we truly fear the Lord, it will make a difference in our lives. I repeat, there will be a change!! We will see sin as God sees it, with His view, with His intolerance, and never compromise His commandments. We will not have our left foot in the Church and our right foot in the world. The fear of the Lord will cause us to have a different attitude toward sin. "The fear of the Lord is to hate evil: pride, and arrogancy, and the evil way, and the froward mouth, do I hate" (Proverbs 8:13).

A good sign of spiritual maturity certainly will be displayed by a life that has learned to fear His name. When we begin to reach this level of maturity, we will begin to see our sinful struggles dissolve. It won't be so great of a struggle to serve the Lord. We will begin to see the blessings of God manifested in our lives. Serving God is not burdensome. It is delightful.

The Lord never expects from us what He won't give us the grace, ability and strength to carry out. I repeat God will not bring that person, that situation, that opportunity into your life without providing a way to attain it. Stop grumbling about "Little Miss Pain in the Butt"; she might have been brought into your life by divine appointment! God might have sent her there to teach you something.

If someone comes walking into your life who seems to want to unload a lot of burdens on you, God has already gone ahead and supplied the grace for you to be able to minister to them. It might not be the kind of help that they want, maybe they are looking for money or for attention, when what the Lord really wants you to share with them is some TLC, or some Godly wisdom or chastisement.

It took me many years into my adulthood to learn that the fear of the Lord is more important than the fear of man. Ask anyone who has known me for any length of time, I've paid a huge price for having such a strong dose of the fear of man. I was much more concerned about man's reaction to what I did than God's reaction. "What would they think? What would they say?" God forbid that Little Miss Goodie Two Shoes should ever be caught in a wrong doing! God, in His awesome love and mercy, would forgive me in an instant at my request, but man would have something to talk about for decades! And guilt would destroy me before I would ever come to forgive myself. My mind continually entertained the fear of what people thought of me. The torment of fear far outweighed the consequence of anything I ever said or did.

But God's grace has been rich in my life. I have finally come to grips with Matthew 10:28: "Fear not them which kill the body, but are not able to kill the soul: but rather fear him which is able to destroy both soul and body in hell." Life is so much more relaxing. There's a peace that comes only from being free from the scars that the fear of man produces in our lives!

I realized that I had truly matured in the fear of the Lord when the day came that I could honestly cry out to God and say, "Whatever it takes, save my family members, Lord. Be it poverty, famine, sickness, disease, tragedy or even death," and I meant every word of it. I knew my faith in God had really blossomed when I reached this point in my life.

It shouldn't have surprised me when just two to three weeks later I got a phone call that my dad, who had had an on/off relationship with the Lord all of his life, had recommitted his life to the Lord. Another three weeks went by, and I got another phone call, on a Sunday evening right in the middle of a tornado watch. "Guess what happened tonight?" I'm thinking, "I don't know Mom. Did a tornado knock the steeple off your church?" Well, I was close! The winds of the Holy Ghost swept through their church and filled my father with the Holy Ghost on Pentecost Sunday 1998. Bless God! I have prayed earnestly for over 20 years, "Lord, if you never do another thing for me, save my dad and help him to develop a steadfast relationship with you." My dad is now a different person. There is a whole new disposition about him. He has really mellowed out. There is a radiance about him.

He had come close a number of times before but always regressed to his old ways. That night, a true change had taken place in his heart, soul, mind, thoughts and actions. Repentance that led to a difference! He learned that lukewarm Christianity isn't Christianity, and he did something about it! His motive was now pure and honorable before God. God saw that he was serious and meant business.

You see God looks on our hearts; He sees our motives. His thoughts and ways are higher than ours. What is your motive for serving the Church, for sharing needs, for praise and worship? Is it to be seen of man? What is your motive for going to the altar? To be noticed by someone? To get the attention of the minister so he'll come by and pray you through? To seek the pity of a lady friend who might come by and give you the opportunity to share your woes? To use God now that you're in a mess?

Are you sorry for the wrong in your life or are you sorry that you got caught? Are you ready to repent and give up your sinful nature or are you sorry for the mess it has you in?

What is your motive for serving in the Church? To get your name in the bulletin? Would you do the same task if the pastor never took notice? It's amazing how many people make a pastor or an evangelist their god. They need a minister to pray them through, teach them about the Bible, give them a frequent pep talk, visit their sick family members, but they never develop a relationship with God themselves.

You see a right relationship with God produces a change of heart, it requires humility before God and man. Restitutions will take place; things will be made right. There will be a difference in our speech and our actions.

We are now marveling at the Move of God across our land as God is pouring out His Spirit upon all flesh. Revival is sweeping through churches all over America and all around the world. Those who earnestly have sought for a change in their heart and soul are the ones who are experiencing this mighty move.

It is occurring in the lives of countless Christians who didn't want to miss out on what God is doing in the Last Days. It is happening in those who have surrendered their all to Him and repented of any known fault. They've asked God to cleanse them from every sin and set them free. No single evangelist or man can bring revival to your church or town. It needs to take place in your own life. It lies within yourself.

Notes

[1]*Children's Letters To God* compiled by Stuart Hample and Eric Marshall (Workman Publishing, 1991).

4
Rooted!

"He shall be like a tree planted by the rivers of water" (Psalm 1:3).

By now, we've clearly learned how vitally important it is for us to keep pure and clean, holy before the Lord. Win the lost at all costs. No time for compromise. Sold out for the cause of the Gospel. On Christ the solid rock I stand, all other ground is sinking sand. How do we begin to attain holiness before our Maker? Through a good dose of the fear of the Lord and staying rooted.

I thank God continuously for the impression that He put in my heart at just 14 years of age. Being raised in the Church all of my life, by a God-fearing mother, I had the opportunity through several Bible Clubs to memorize large portions of Scripture at a very young age. I'll never forget when I was around 14 years old, I was in my room meditating on the warnings of the deception in the end times as given in Matthew, chapter 24. A good dose of the fear of the Lord was rooted in my soul as I read of the great falling away of many in the Last Days. Right then and there, I *determined* to stay clean before Him all of the days of my life, that I not be caught in a "slip up" at the day of His appearing. This commitment has stuck with me ever since and has kept me in my Christian walk through the storms of life.

I took the Lord's plea to *endure till the end* very seriously, and it has always carried me through. Faith that came by hearing the Word of God was planted into my being! When all else crumbled before me, this commitment stuck with me. When troubles from every side, persecutions, hurts, disappointments galore, insecurities, the fiery trials of life came in like a flood, I remained planted, immovable in Christ Jesus, steadfast and rooted in Him.

"Therefore, my beloved brethren, be ye stedfast, unmoveable, always abounding in the work of the Lord, forasmuch as ye know that your labour is not in vain in the Lord" (I Corinthians 15:58).

Let us say with the apostle Paul that nothing has separated us from a steadfast relationship with Him.

"Who shall separate us from the love of Christ? Shall tribulation, or distress, or persecution or famine, or nakedness, or peril, or sword? As it is written, For thy sake we are killed all the day long; we are accounted as sheep for the slaughter. Nay in all these things we are more than conquerors through him that loved us. For I am persuaded, that neither death, nor life, nor angels, nor principalities, nor powers, nor things present, nor things to come, nor height, nor depth, nor any other creature, shall be able to separate us from the love of God, which is in Christ Jesus our Lord" (Romans 8:35-39).

Why? How? I repeat, I **determined** to remain steadfast and rooted in Him who I believed all of the days of my life! I was like a tree planted by the water – immovable!

"Nevertheless the foundation of God standeth sure, having this seal, The Lord knoweth them that are his. And, Let every one that nameth the name of Christ depart from iniquity" (11 Timothy 2:19).

What a powerful verse. I never took notice of this verse before, but just recently it jumped off the page at me. This is my testimony, I have a seal. I am His!

Do you think I take my security in Christ for granted for a moment? No never!! As I look around, there are those who come to Christ with good intentions to serve Him with unswerving faith everywhere. People are in and out of church nowadays like clothing that goes in and out of style. Even Paul in his writings rebuked the Galatians for so soon being removed from the Gospel.

"I marvel that ye are so soon removed from him that called you into the grace of Christ unto another gospel" (Galatians 1:6).

We must persevere, be determined to make it at all costs.

It is so important we teach our young people the importance of a personal relationship with Jesus Christ. They can't get to heaven on their grandmother's religion or their father's strong faith in Christ. Each individual has to experience it first-hand for themselves. Remember that I was only 14 years old at the time of this life-changing experience.

I was also 14 when God impressed upon my heart that I would someday be a writer. He spoke to me while I was sitting in my country church one evening, after learning of the tragic drowning of a toddler in the community. I was struggling with strong emotions, and the Lord spoke to me and told me that someday He would take this young, shy introverted teenager and use me mightily to express my inward feelings and convictions by way of writing. We need to be careful not to under-estimate the power of God in the lives of our youngsters.

We need to impress upon our youth the need to have a daily walk with the Lord and keep rooted in Him. It will keep them pure and holy throughout their teenage years and inspire them to keep their eyes on Him. Start praying for your youngsters, well before they hit their teens, that God will raise up a Godly spouse for them, someone who is also rooted in a one-on-one relationship with the Lord.

God Is In Control!

I began by testifying of God's power in my life as a teenager. Let me conclude this chapter by sharing His faithfulness to me throughout my adult life. God, in His rich mercy, allowed me to walk through some high waters of life so I would learn to trust in His great wisdom.

My oldest child reached his adolescent years with a bang. The middle child was in elementary school, and the youngest one was in what seemed to be terrible twos extended. I was working three part-time jobs. I started having health problems after health problems. I would no sooner get a lick on one problem and another one would erupt. Every problem just snowballed another. I was physically and emotionally drained.

After about four years of being stretched to the limit, I was hoping for a period of rest. Life needed to slow down for me, but every time I thought I could see the light at the end of the tunnel, all hope was pulled out from under me. Just when I thought that things were starting to run a little more smoothly, the bottom fell out.

The first six weeks of 1996 brought with them unusual headaches in my temples, around my eyes. I tried to pass them off as a combination of sinus problems and stress, but things seemed quite strange. Something just didn't seem quite right.

Then, one Sunday evening, February 18, 1996, it happened! I laid down on the couch to relax and was struck by a severe, piercing headache in my left temple. Something seemed desperately wrong. After about 40 minutes of intense pain, I shifted positions and it subsided.

The following week, I suffered spasms along the left side of my face and felt really strange. Monday morning, I went to work feeling extremely stressed, like something terrible was about to take place. The doctor I worked for just about flipped out when he noticed the unusually large unequal dilation of my left pupil.

I was rushed through numerous tests beginning with glaucoma, an MRI of the brain for what they thought was a tumor, an arteriogram to rule out an aneurysm, diabetes testing and other numerous considerations. Shifted from specialist to specialist, I was told anything from I probably had a tumor, to it could be my heart, to "Oh, you were probably just born that way and are just now noticing"!?!

Nevertheless, all tests came back negative, and it was finally diagnosed that an infection had set in and caused long-term nerve damage. It was a very traumatic experience to say the least and my faith was put to the test. I went through a great range of highs and lows emotionally, but the night that still stands out in my mind as though it was yesterday was the night that I made the initial visit to the doctor's office.

After being told I'd first have to have an MRI of the brain to rule out a tumor, I drove away feeling overwhelmed by the powers of darkness and despair. "Now, what am I going to do, Lord?" I wailed.

As quickly as I questioned the Lord, supernatural strength came over me. I remembered what a former pastor had always impressed upon me: "God is in control" of everything. When things are going good, He's in the midst, when the storms arise, He's still God! Though I always was a pessimist, I spoke with confidence, "I'm going to serve the Lord with what little strength I have left in my body for whatever time I have left on this earth. I will spend it serving God with all that is within me." I meant every word that I spoke.

When I got home, I shared with my husband, cried and prayed. By the time I went to bed, the only thing that I asked the Lord was, "Please, let me get some sleep tonight; don't let me suffer with severe insomnia." I went to bed and, surprisingly, was sleeping well before midnight.

Well, about 3:00 a.m., after about four hours of sleep, I suddenly awoke. I felt like I had been sleeping for ten hours! I sat straight up in my bed; the glory of God filled the room. There was an excitement in the air! What was the wonderful news that I had received just before bedtime? Oh... yeah, the doctor told me I might have a brain tumor. But, the peace of God that passeth all understanding overwhelmed me. I didn't have a peace that everything was going to be alright. I had a joy that God was in control despite the circumstance. He would be God through all things, in spite of the outcome.

The words of a song I had just learned a few days earlier rang in my ears: "Every road I've traveled down, you have walked before me, you made the light to shine out of darkness. I am looking for the day when I bow before You, lay my crown down at Your feet." I was so overwhelmed by the presence of God that I jumped out of bed, ran into the kitchen and cupped my hand over my mouth to sing the song before I awoke my husband and he'd kill me before the brain tumor did!

Three months later, before I sang a duet in church – "Every road I've traveled down, You have walked before me...," I testified with full confidence in my God. "God is looking for a people who will serve Him in spite of their infirmities. For better or for worse, for richer or for poorer, in sickness and in health, *even* in death we *won't* part!!"

No, not even death can separate me from the love of God.

"For if I live, I live unto the Lord, if I die, I die unto the Lord. If I live, therefore, or die, I am the Lord's" (Romans 14:8). "For to me to live is Christ, and to die is gain" (Philippians 1:21).

5
The Eye of a Needle

"It is easier for a camel to go through the eye of a needle, than for a rich man to enter into the kingdom of God" (Matthew 19:24).

We live in a very materialistic day and age. Everything we do and every place we go costs us something. The price we pay just for our basic livelihood has become outrageous. Food and clothing come with high price tags. Our automobiles and houses practically own us. And, if the basics don't do us in, insurances and taxes will!

Our children and youth today are no longer content with a coloring book and crayons. A bouncing ball just doesn't keep their attention any longer than it takes to get it out of the toy box. We are exposed to more entertainment than ever, yet we remain less content than at any other time in history. We never seem to reach a level of satisfaction anymore. Before we ever attain one goal, we move on to dream about the next. Our lives are filled with things.

We feed on junk. The foods we eat usually contain little or no nutritional value. Every function we attend, every fast food restaurant, every food and beverage machine on the sidewalk usually offers at our disposal fast, easy junk foods. Chips, pretzels, soda, pizza, crackers, cake and ice cream are what we fill up on. They are our quick fix to hold our stomachs over in our fast-paced world. We feed our bodies on things that have no nutritional benefit, and our spirits on things of no eternal value whatsoever.

The old saying, "Money isn't everything but it sure does help," hits home. Let's face it – sometimes we feel like money *can* pay for anything. What is our punishment for exceeding the speed limit? A fine! How can the newly arrested convict dish his way out? Bail money! How do we beautify our physical body? Spend some cash and get that make-over! Apart from an excellent insurance benefit, it is almost impossible to get adequate health care nowadays. Money talks!

We all dream of that financial miracle that will clean our slate, but do the well-to-do find in the end that it was worth it? We hear all of the time of individuals who won the lottery and a few years later went under. Statistics have proven that the upper income class is less likely to be dependent on God than the lower and middle class are.

Riches have little or no eternal value. In fact, they tend to do more damage than good in too many situations. They tend to cloud our view of the eternal picture.

"For what shall it profit a man, if he shall gain the whole world, and lose his own soul? Or what shall a man give in exchange for his soul?" (Mark 8:36,37).

Have you ever fantasized in your mind what you would do if you got your dream come true of sudden wealth? Have those thoughts ever ventured on to the end result? Less dependency on God, more responsibility, more expectations from people. Sounds like a big headache in the ultimate end.

Looking back over the years of my marriage, I reflect upon significant financial struggles. I had to trust God many times when I could not trust my wallet. Through it all, my faith has been enriched. Today I can truly say, I am thankful that I did not ever have the riches this world has to offer. Would I be as strong in the Lord if this had not been the case?

"Labour not to be rich: cease from thine own wisdom. Wilt thou set thine eyes upon that which is not? For riches certainly make themselves wings; they fly away as an eagle toward heaven" (Proverbs 23:4-5). How interesting! Even Solomon was able to warn us of the emptiness that filling our lives with materialism leads to. Things simply are made to decay.

We need to hold claim on the little saying we see on plaques, "Only one life will soon be passed, only what's done for Christ will last." What an awesome truth. We can't take it with us!

The apostle Peter, in I Peter 1:18, reminds us that "We are not redeemed with corruptible things as silver and gold."

The Lord has brought me a long way in the area of faith. He has shown me that a lack of believing that our needs as a family would be met is reflecting a lack of faith in Him. He has promised to provide for His own!

Of course, there is a price to pay. We must be faithful stewards of the blessings God has bestowed upon us, and live by His principles. "But seek ye first the kingdom of God, and His righteousness, and all these things shall be added unto you" (Matthew 6:33).

Though we know beyond a doubt that riches don't bring happiness into our lives, it never ceases to amaze me how much emphasis we put on them. I've often won-dered why there are three classes of people – upper class, middle class and lower class. Why couldn't every-one make the same basic income? Besides, we all have the same basic needs for food, clothing, insurance and housing.

When my two oldest children were preschoolers, I was blessed with being able to stay at home with them during those impressionable years. By the time the third child came along, things were a lot different. Money was tighter and needs were greater. I tried work-ing from my home, but things did not work out for long, and I was forced back into the work world.

I went through a lot of hard-core struggles over the next five years, trying to balance work with motherhood, church activities and all the responsibilities of home-making that we have as ladies. There were a number of times I was near the point of a nervous breakdown. My stress level during this period of time in my life was at its peak. It didn't seem hardly worth it; the more money you make the more bills you have and the more you tend to spend. Anxiety was often overwhelming, and it's inter-esting to note that this was the same time frame in my life that I was bombarded with health problems!

When that long awaited day came that I could leave the workplace to work out of my home again, everything and everybody around me suddenly seemed to change! Everybody else seemed so much kinder. The kids didn't seem to be so high strung after all. Life seemed to come at a more relaxing pace. I really mellowed out. I became living proof of how different life can be in a more simple, cozy lifestyle.

I grew in leaps and bounds spiritually and emotionally in just a few short months. I now had quality time
to dig into the Word, pray without ceasing, intercede
and take time to smell the roses. The Lord did so many
supernatural miracles, far above all that I could ask or
think. Grocery shopping and budgeting seemed so much
easier. Household projects didn't seem like an impossible dream after all.

I became in control of my house, instead of my house
being in control of me. It was no longer a house, but a
home, a haven of rest. The joy of motherhood was
restored to me. The Lord restored that which the
cankerworm stole from me. There was a fresh appreciation for the simple things of life. He had simply been
waiting for me to trust Him all along. I was amazed at
how He worked on my behalf when I stepped out in obedience to His Will for my life. He gave me the desires of
my heart.

When we hear the verse that the Lord will give us
the desires of our heart, we take it that He will give us
anything we want if we ask and add His name to it.
Maybe, what really is meant by this verse is that God
will place His desires for our lives on our heart as we
grow spiritually. When we learn to live by what He
intends for our life, instead of continually struggling and
striving for our wishes and dreams, life becomes so much
more relaxing. Peace and joy saturates our beings.

When I put my trust into the hand of the Living
God, I felt like my life was splashed with a fresh new
paint job. I felt like a whole new person – body, soul and
spirit. God closed many doors in my life and opened up
windows!

Creation or Creator?

I want to finish this chapter with a poem that I wrote when I was in my mid-teens. I found myself struggling with insecurity, as many young people do. I was overcome by feelings of inferiority, as I was always finding people who were able to outdo my very best talents.

In my despair, I laid down in bed one night and the Lord revealed some powerful insights to me. He reminded me that He was also rejected of men and how He created the world but now man serves the creation more than the creator (Romans 11:25). It was at this time, this poem was given to me by the divine anointing of the Lord.

The Creator

I've always been a person,
With a big imagination,
I dreamed I could accomplish great things,
But I only caused all this frustration.

I would write the best song,
Sing the prettiest melody,
Date the hot shot of the town,
And live in harmony.

I thought I deserved to reach great things,
But was only in my fantasies,
For the things I would come up with,
Had been around for centuries.

Jealousy overwhelmed me,
For others started to excel,
And do good from the beginning,
In things I thought I do so well.

But then one day it struck me,
When lying down to sleep,
God came in that still small voice,
And said something to this sheep.

"My Child," He said,
"You have My heart,
Heaven and earth have *I* created,
Yet men try to do *My* part.

"Do not think you must be perfect,
I am the only one,
You are unique while here on earth,
And someday... you'll be like My Son."

Twas a disappointing moment,
For all of my life I had believed,
I must be best in everything,
Boy, was I ever deceived!

The Bible tells me not to covet,
What others have been given,
Just do your best with what you have,
And enjoy the way *you're* livin'.

Now I realize that I am special,
And considered to be great value,
Yet no better than any other,
Just one of God's chosen few.

Do not take my poem lightly,
Tis my life story you see,
But now I understand more,
Who Jesus deserves to be.

6

The Devil...
SIN Made Me Do It!

"For all have sinned, and come short of the glory of God" (Romans 3:23).

"The devil made me do it!" is a very familiar statement to most of us. Most of us realize it is also the biggest scapegoat we tend to use. How can the devil make us do anything? He can only play on our weaknesses. Take a look at the word *sin*, the man in the middle is "I." "I have sinned, Lord."

We spend our lives looking for someone to blame for all of our faults and all of our problems. If it isn't the devil we are trying to push fault on, it is our parents or our spouse, or maybe even our children. We all should have the middle name of "Adam." He tried as hard as he could to blame his wife, Eve, but he eventually had to face the fact that the end result was that the man in the mirror was "me."

There are so many Scriptures written on sin and its consequences. The Bible tells us more about hell than it does about heaven. The Lord must be so caring for us that he doesn't want any one of us to be eternally damned.

This chapter is going to involve an intense amount of Scriptures on this sensitive subject. There is so much to say about this ugly word *sin*, but I cannot begin to say anything more or anything less than what God has already said in His Word. I dare not add to or take away from anything He has already said on such a serious matter.

Man has a tendency to exaggerate and overstate what was intended from the beginning, and even more often, we see a trend to eliminate or sugar coat the holiness of God's nature. We tend to excuse the little idols that creep into our lives so subtly. We tend to cover up for others and try to explain their ill behavior by stating they are simply going through a rough time and have too much stress on them.

The Word of God is an offense to those who are not living by it. None of us like to have our toes stepped on. We get all bent out of shape when someone reminds us that we are less than perfect. Holiness is something that God requires of us. I, the author of this book, did not come up with it on my own. Father God from the beginning of time created man to live by His standards and to follow His principles.

God, calls us to holiness everyday. It matters not whether we woke up on the wrong side of the bed or whether it's convenient to live right today. We have a responsibility to keep up our guard from the devices of the enemy.

Another statement you often hear is, "Look what the devil is trying to do – He's been on me all day." No doubt, the devil is on the prey full force to look for open windows in our lives.

"Little children, let no man deceive you: he that doeth righteousness is righteous, even as he is righteous. He that committeth sin is of the devil, for the devil sinneth from the beginning. For this purpose the Son of God was manifested, that he might destroy the works of the devil." (I John 3:7,8).

I still believe most that dilemmas we find ourselves in, usually are a result of our own planting. We see how far we can go and get away with it, and before long, we find ourselves in too deep. We tend to keep "bugging God," hoping that He will change His mind and give in. We're like little kids. Two of my three children are very strong-willed, and I often find myself telling them, "No matter how many times you ask, the answer is still going to be *no*." Then to be cute, I go on to add, "But if you ask one more time, you're in trouble." Do we actually think that if we keep hounding God, he will give in and permit us to participate in that which He designed as wrong since the beginning of time?

When we begin to see sin as God sees it, we will understand the seriousness of its nature. We need to picture it with His big camera. There are heavy consequences involved, both in this life and the life to come. Thank God for His mercy that we still have time to ask Him to erase our slate while we're still in this life.

What an impact there would be on our lives if we literally put to practice the exhortation in the ninth chapter of Mark: "And if thy hand offend thee, cut if off: it is better for thee to enter into life maimed, than having two hands to go into hell, into the fire that never shall be quenched: Where their worm dieth not, and the fire is not quenched. And if thy foot offend thee, cut it off: it is better for thee to enter halt into life, than having two feet to be cast into hell, into the fire that never shall be quenched: Where their worm dieth not, and the fire is not quenched. And if thine eye offend thee, pluck it out: it is better for thee to enter into the kingdom of God with one eye, than having two eyes to be cast into hell fire" (Mark 9:43-47).

What a powerful passage of Scripture. I don't think most of us would have many body parts left if we took this Scripture to heart; or, maybe we would actually take the issue more serious and think before we act.

It never ceases to amaze me how often we pray for God to answer our prayers and to bless us as we know He desires to do, but continue to harbor sin in our lives. It may seem like a simple sin to us, maybe that of rebellion or unforgiveness, or maybe we have some hidden idols in our heart. There is a price to pay in this Christian walk. We have principles to follow as we continue to grow spiritually.

If you do "those things, which ye have both learned, and received, and heard, and seen in me, then the God of peace shall be with you" (Philippians 4:9). We can't just assume that since we attend church and know all about God, He is going to magically overlook our evil and bless us anyway. We need to learn and put to practice what we've learned; then Godly benefits will come with it.

"If I regard iniquity in my heart, the Lord will not hear me" (Psalms 66:18). There is a procedure for coming before the throne of God. It involves first seeking forgiveness and cleansing for all that has crept into our lives that is not pleasing in His sight, then thanksgiving offered for His great love. From there, we can proceed to ask Him for His favor in areas of our lives that we need help in and healing in, be it body, soul or spirit.

The Scriptures make it clear that when we choose to disobey, the Lord's blessings are withheld from us. Answers to prayers come when a righteous person is practicing the right things, in right standing with God, with right condition of heart, submitting to God's right timing and right plan for his or her life. We are called to be righteous people, not wishy washy spiritually.

God does not compromise His commands. He does not tolerate the act of sin in the camp. Where one church member sins, it affects the whole body. If your toe was infected, wouldn't your whole body suffer? We must realize the seriousness that our evil practices play on the whole Body of Christ.

"For as by one man's disobedience many were made sinners, so by the obedience of one shall many be made righteous" (Romans 5:19).

We often get so set in our ways and so used to doing the things that we always have, that after a while, we don't even recognize it as sin anymore. What was once obviously uncomfortable for us to participate in, just doesn't seem so hard anymore. We've become immune to the effects of sin. With the widespread use of abortions, as well as rape and murder in our world, we just don't remember that at one time these things were almost unheard of. They are no longer all that devastating – we are so used to hearing nothing but garbage and tragedy on the news.

It is like when our bodies get ill with disease. Sometimes we suffer for weeks, months or even years before a diagnosis is finally made. We wonder how we could have been sick for so long without even knowing how sick we were.

My gallbladder surgery was an excellent example of this. I was only in my mid-twenties when I seemed to experience a lot of stomach queasiness. Otherwise, I really didn't have any obvious or drastic symptoms. In 1990, however, I started to have an occasional strange episode of severe abdominal pain and vomiting. The pain would pass as fast as it came, so I never went to the emergency room.

I expressed my concern to my doctor several times at routine visits, and he replied that I probably had something viral going on. Then, one day early in October, I not only experienced a lot of queasiness, I felt like someone's fist was punching me right in the liver area. It was not so intense that I could not stand it, but it did not go away, so I made a doctor appointment.

I went to the doctor's office that Wednesday evening not thinking that anything too serious was wrong. That was until he asked me to give a urine sample. I pointed out what he already saw was obvious. My urine was an orangish black color. "What could that be from?" I asked. "Well, Joy, chances are it is coming from gall-stones or advanced gall disease, and if this is the case, surgery will be necessary. I will send you for an x-ray first thing in the morning."

I went home, finished up the laundry and packed a few necessities just in case they decided to keep me. I still didn't take the matter all that serious; after all, I had been told for the prior two years that I simply had a lot of stomach viruses. I guess I thought if something drastic was wrong, I would be doubled over with unbearable pain. When my mother had her gallbladder attack, we practically had to carry her to the doctor.

That Thursday morning I drove myself to the radiology department at the hospital, telling my husband I would call him at work when I got the results. I wasn't back in the waiting room very long after the testing until my family doctor met me with the results. I had dozens of gallstones the size of peas, and one was stuck tight in my bile duct, making surgery absolutely necessary. He told me to go admit myself to the emergency room right away until a surgeon could be reached to come talk to me.

I agreed, but just about floored the doctor when I asked if I could I could just walk across the street to the store for a few minutes first to pick up a few things for my hospital stay. I had no idea how critical a shape I was actually in! Besides, people put off gallbladder surgery for months and even years. What was the big hurry? I just didn't get it.

Ten to fifteen minutes later when I returned to the emergency room, the doctor was pacing the floor. "Where is your husband?" one of the nurses asked.

"Well, I was going to wait until I got the official report from the surgeon and then call him at work with the news."

"No! You don't want to do that. You are scheduled for emergency surgery immediately, as soon as the surgeon arrives."

A few minutes later, my husband came in, and the surgeon arrived, apologizing that he took so long. My, everyone seemed in such a rush. They acted like I was dying. Well, I was. The surgeon went on to explain:

"Normally, gallbladder surgery is something that can be planned, something that gives you have a choice in the matter. You, however, have a stone stuck tight in your bile duct and have developed a low grade fever. You have no choice in the matter. Emergency surgery is in order. It is now shortly after lunch; if we wait as long as supper time, it may be too late. The advanced disease may get into your bloodstream. We don't believe it is too late yet, but we can't say for certain."

I was possibly dying, and the only symptoms that made it obvious was the feeling of being kicked just below my middle chest area, along with the abnormal color of my urine sample. I had been sick for so long that I was immune to any other warning symptoms that may have been present.

Unbelievable, but true. Unfortunately, millions of people are the same way in their spiritual life. They have been sin-stained for so long that they don't even recognize the warning signs that God places in their path. They are so diseased by this world's evil nature that they don't even know the difference.

Maybe, they are even in church every single Sunday but still drinking from the bottle. They refuse to go deeper into the things of God and live by His principles. They become stifled in their growth and spiritually sick, and they eventually die to the things of God. To stay alive spiritually, we must feed our souls daily just like we do our physical bodies.

"Know ye not that the unrighteous shall not inherit the kingdom of God? Be not deceived: neither fornicators, nor idolaters, nor adulterers, nor effeminate, nor abusers of themselves with mankind, Nor thieves, nor covetous, nor drunkards, nor revilers, nor extortioners, shall inherit the kingdom of God. And such were some of you: **BUT** ye are washed, but ye are sanctified, but ye are justified in the name of the Lord Jesus, and by the Spirit of our God" (I Corinthians 6:9-11).

Getting Down to the Nitty Gritty

Some sins are obvious: Do not steal, kill, commit fornication, go to the bars or take drugs. They were the common things that we were preached about when I was in my adolescence. Today they almost seem like the least of the "Thou shall nots." There are so many more things to deal with nowadays when it comes to raising teenagers.

These are still the big ones with the heavier consequences, but we are told in God's Holy Word that He is coming for a church without spot or wrinkle. We are to totally surrender our lives to Him. Before God, sin is sin, and all needs to be dealt with.

Let's focus on the things that subtly sneak into the lives of church people, those who think they are not vulnerable to fall. Before we can effectively minister to the lost, we need to make sure that we are in right standing with God ourselves.

"For the time is come that judgment must begin at the house of God: and if it first begin at us, what shall the end be of them that obey not the gospel of God?" (I Peter 4:17).

Pride

This type of person is easy to spot. Every time you converse with them, you hear, "I this and I that." PrIde with a capital *I* in the middle is all over them. They take credit for everybody and everything that was ever accomplished. They are wiser in their eyes than God Himself. No one can do anything without them, at least not anything right.

They make sure that everyone notices all of their good works too. They are the ones that are sure that their names make the bulletin and everyone knows what they have achieved this week. When giving prayer requests, they even throw in how good they've been to Uncle Henry who really needs lifting up.

It goes back to what we learned in chapter one about testing the spirits by the fruit of their mouth. Their words are filled with self-centeredness.

"Take heed that ye do not your alms before men, to be seen of them: otherwise ye have no reward of your Father which is in heaven" (Matthew 6:1).

A proud look is at the top of the list of things that the Lord hates (Proverbs 6:16-19). Imagine that the Lord Himself states point blank that He actually *hates* pride.

"For whosoever exalteth himself shall be abased; and he that humbleth himself shall be exalted" (Luke 14:11).

Rebellion and Stubbornness

Rebellion and stubbornness go hand in hand. People who are often very stubborn when it comes to cooperating with anything or anybody, tend to be rebellious toward authority. Let's remember that what appears to be rebellion toward people and church leaders and government authorities, is really, more likely than not, a reflection of a heart condition of rebellion toward God Himself.

Every church has someone, at least one person that is sitting in it, that you just can't please no matter how hard you seem to try. They complain about everything and everybody. As soon as some zealous saint wants to do something awesome for the work of the Lord, their rebellious nature arrives on the scene. Very vocal people of course, disputing what you are doing, how you are doing it and why do you think you need to be doing such a thing.

They appear to be very stubborn toward letting anyone but themselves run the show. They appear not to like you very well, but in the ultimate end, if truth be known, they are really rebelling toward God Himself. They know that God laid that thing on your heart for you to do, and they are opposed to what God chose to do in the Church through you.

"For rebellion is as the sin of witchcraft, and stubbornness is as iniquity and idolatry. Because thou has rejected the word of the Lord, he hath also rejected thee from being king" (I Samuel 15:23). Listen to that! We always hear the first part of that verse, but listen to what the last half says. The very thing that I pointed out in the previous paragraph "Because thou has rejected the word of the Lord, he hath also rejected *thee* from being king."

Self-righteousness

These are the people who think they have "arrived" in the things of God – they are God's perfection on earth. No one else can do the work of the Lord better than they can.

These are the ones who act like they think that they are smarter than God Himself. Follow *their* good example, and you will make it in the pearly gates.

"Jesus said unto him, I am the way, the truth, and the life: no man cometh unto the Father, but by me" (John 14:6).

They better move over when God moves in and crucify some pride!

Criticism

Critical, complaining, mumble, mumble, grumble, grumble, nag, nag, gripe, gripe. How awful, yet one of the hardest things for our human nature to overcome. We are exposed to so much negativism every day of our lives that we just fall right into the trap ourselves. Negative words and feelings are always coming out of our mouths.

Not very edifying, but let the truth be spoken. The devil just loves it! If he can get God's people to grumble, he has it made. It does nothing but tear down a family, including the church family. Once there's division and hurt in the church, he has his foot in the door.

"Do all things without murmurings and disputings" (Philippians 2:14).

Gossip

That all too common problem, especially among women. We are the most competitive creatures that God ever made. We always need to find fault with the next so that we can make ourselves feel a little better. We just can't stand for anyone else to get ahead of us. We spend our lives comparing ourselves to the next lady. We are possessed with a holier than thou type of attitude.

Being such jealous beings, we really can get our tongues in trouble. "Did you hear about Mrs. Smith? I just can't believe that she did that! Well, she always was a different type of person. No wonder her kids turned out the way they did, having a mother like that. Now we know what she's really like. We should have known better than to trust her."

Sometimes, we get a little more tactful with our gossip. "I need to ask you to pray with me. I have a real concern. Mrs. Smith really needs my prayers and yours too. Do you know that she ...da, da, da, da da," and on we go to proceed to tell all the gossip we know or that we think we know about Mrs. Smith. Until it's all said and done, that person passes it to just one more person and then on to just one more, and before you know it, it gets repeated back to you much more intensely than what you ever mentioned. The story you once told was taken and shared, exaggerated and overstated, then some more facts eliminated and repeated out of context until the whole story was totally out of proportion to what it originally began as.

There is no way possible that Person #1 even had all of the details 100 percent correct, unless she was the one it happened to or unless she was God herself. Even if we repeated something that happened to us personally, some miscommunication might have taken place between ourselves and the other party.

The devil loves to work through miscommunication. Just let someone get their feelings hurt, and it breeds and festers into something significant in our minds, when some of the facts were just taken or given totally out of proper perspective to begin with.

If it doesn't pertain to you, keeping out of other people's matters will save you a lot of headaches in the long run.

"But let none of you suffer as a murderer, or as a thief, or as an evildoer, or as a busybody in other men's matters" (I Peter 4:15).

Unforgiveness

"For if ye forgive men their trespasses, your heavenly Father will also forgive you: But if ye forgive not men their trespasses, neither will your Father forgive your trespasses" (Matthew 6:14,15).

Oh, the blessedness of having mercy on others as God has shown mercy toward us. If we would only remember where we came from ourselves and what God has brought us through, it would save us a lot of headaches obtained from the unwillingness to forgive. Probably a lot of ulcers and illnesses too.

None of us are immune from falling into sin. All mankind is vulnerable. When our brother sins against us, we need to forgive as Christ forgave and welcome him back to the family with open arms.

When we fail to forgive those who trespass against us, we often turn bitter, and the end often results in us doing the same horrible thing that we could not forgive someone else for. We become just like them.

Judgmental

"Judge not, that ye be not judged. For with what judgment ye judge, ye shall be judged: and with what measure ye mete, it shall be measured to you again. And why beholdest thou the mote that is in thy brother's eye, but considerest not the beam that is in thine own eye? Or how wilt thou say to thy brother, Let me pull out the mote out of thine eye; and behold, a beam is in thine own eye? Thou hypocrite, first cast out the beam out of thine own eye; and then shalt thou see clearly to cast out the mote out of thy brother's eye" (Matthew 7:1-5).

This very familiar passage really hits home. We just looked at the issue of being critical and how ugly it can become. The things that tend to bug us about the next person, we often have to admit are the very ones that we ourselves struggle with. It is like that person is a reflection of our own shortcomings, and it looks so horrible when we see ourselves in the mirror.

Just listen to the things that people say about each other. Quite often, when we make negative remarks about another person, we describe ourselves to a tee. We all do it. It is a sin common to mankind. We point our index finger at the next guy and fail to realize in doing so, we have the remaining three fingers pointing right back at ourselves.

We will see a great maturity in the Body of Christ when we come to the point in our lives where we can grow up and stop judging our fellow brethren. *If they have fallen*, the last thing they need is someone standing in their face pointing a finger at them. They *know* they have blown it. They now need someone who is mature enough to say, "Hey, so you need some help. Take my hand, let's walk together and talk together and overcome so that we can go on with life."

Jealousy

"A certain man had two sons: And the younger of them said to his father, Father, give me the portion of goods that falleth to me. And he divided unto them his living. And not many days after the younger son gathered all together, and took his journey into a far country, and there wasted his substance with riotous living. And when he had spent all, there arose a mighty famine in that land; and he began to be in want. And he went and joined himself to a citizen of that country; and he sent him into his fields to feed swine. And he would fain have filled his belly with the husks that the swine did eat: and no man gave unto him. And when he came to himself, he said, How many hired servants of my father's have bread enough and to spare, and I perish with hunger! I will arise and go to my father, and will say unto him, Father, I have sinned against heaven and before thee, And am no more worthy to be called thy son: make me as one of thy hired servants. And he arose, and came to his father. But when he was yet a great way off, his father saw him, and had compassion, and ran, and fell on his neck, and kissed him. And the son said unto him, Father, I have sinned against heaven, and in thy sight, and am no more worthy to be called thy son. But the father said to his servants, Bring forth the best robe, and put it on him; and put a ring on his hand, and shoes on his feet: And bring hither the fatted calf, and kill it; and let us eat and be merry: For this my son was dead, and is alive again; he was lost, and is found. And they began to be merry. Now his elder son was in the field: and as he came and drew nigh to the house, he heard musick and dancing. And he called one of the servants, and asked what these things meant. And he said unto him, Thy brother is come; and thy father hath killed the fatted calf, because he had received him safe and sound. And he was angry, and would not go in: therefore came his father out, and entreated him. And he answering said to his father, Lo, these many years do I serve thee, neither transgressed I at any time thy commandment: and yet thou never gavest me a kid, that I might make merry with my friends: but as soon as this thy son was come, which hath devoured thy living with harlots, thou hast killed for him the fatted calf. And he said unto him, Son, thou art ever with me, and all that I have is thine. It was meet that we should make merry, and be glad: for this thy brother was dead, and is alive again; and was lost, and is found" (Luke 15:11-32).

The parable of the Prodigal Son is such an influencing story. Every time I hear it, however, my own anger rises to the surface. I can identify with the jealous brother! Being the youngest in a family of four, I was often the one that the older ones were jealous of. You know how it is, the baby of the family is usually the spoiled one and gets more clothing, more toys and more attention that the older ones.

I grew up with the Miss Goodie Two Shoes reputation. I always had to keep things straight and not let anyone know my hidden faults. I never got into some of the deeper sins that many people fall to in their youth. I had to keep up my reputation.

I would struggle with an intense anger whenever anyone was treated better than someone else who deserved the better treatment. It didn't even have to be me who was the victim of the situation. If I saw another person get less Christmas presents than their siblings, I was irate. If someone got better treatment than his peers, I got all bent out of shape. Anything unfair in this life, whether it came from a non-Christian, a Christian, a parent or a leader, just burned rubber under me. My inward man just couldn't seem to tolerate unfairness.

When I would hear the story of the Prodigal Son, an angry spirit would boil within me that said, "That's unfair. He had a right to be jealous!. He had been the good one and never caused any trouble, and his brother gets special attention. How unfair!"

But look at how the father responded to the jealous son in verses 31 and 32. He said, "Son, thou art ever with me, and all that I have is thine. It was meet that we should make merry, and be glad: for thy brother was dead, and is alive again; and was lost, and is found." Such wisdom! It's the same type of response that Jesus gave when Judas Iscariot criticized Mary for taking a very costly pound of ointment of spikenard and anointed the feet of Jesus, wiping his foot with her hair. Judas was angry, stating that it could have been sold for three hundred pence and given to the poor. But Jesus responded by stating, "The poor always ye have with you; but me ye have not always" (John 12:8).

Lust

"Dearly beloved, I beseech you as strangers and pilgrims, abstain from fleshly lusts, which war against the soul" (I Peter 2:11).

Lust is often a hidden sin of the heart. Sometimes it comes out, and other times people are somewhat effective at keeping it hidden – at least from man. All sin not dealt with will be brought into the open on judgment day.

Once dwelt on for long enough, lust, like all sins, will reap great consequences. What is on the inside eventually comes out in one form or another. Adultery always begins in the heart. It doesn't just happen. First, it is conceived within the heart of a person, nursed on in the mind, and then, if not dealt with, it could result in devastating consequences.

"For the weapons of our warfare are not carnal, but mighty through God to the pulling down of strong holds; Casting down imaginations, and every high thing that exalteth itself against the knowledge of God, and bringing into captivity every thought to the obedience of Christ" (II Corinthians 10:4,5). We are to cast down those imaginations before they are nurtured in our minds.

Unclean Thoughts

"Let the wicked forsake his way, and the unrighteous man his thoughts: and let him return unto the Lord, and he will have mercy upon him; and to our God, for he will abundantly pardon" (Isaiah 55:7).

Lust is not the only thing that develops in the mind. All sin begins there. Stealing, killing and substance abuse are all thought upon before they happen.

"O generation of vipers, how can ye, being evil, speak good things? For out of the abundance of the heart the mouth speaketh. A good man out of the good treasure of the heart bringeth forth good things: and an evil man out of the evil treasure bringeth forth evil things. But I say unto you, That every idle word that men shall speak, they shall give account thereof in the day of judgment. For by thy words thou shalt be justified, and by thy words thou shalt be condemned" (Matthew 12:34-37).

What we say is rooted on the inside! It is so important to keep our minds stayed upon Jehovah. When we feed upon the wrong things, it's "junk in and junk out." The one rotten apple in one's life will soon spoil the good.

"Let the words of my mouth, and the meditation of my heart, be acceptable in thy sight, O Lord, my strength, and my redeemer" (Psalms 19:14).

Covetousness and Enviousness

"Thou shalt not covet thy neighbor's house, thou shalt not covet thy neighbor's wife, nor his manservant, nor his maidservant, nor his ox, nor his ass, nor any thing that is thy neighbor's" (Exodus 20:17).

Maybe, if we were to be honest, behind most sins the hidden problem is covetousness. Look back over the list that we just studied: Pride, rebellion, self-righteousness, criticism, gossip, unforgiveness, being judgmental, jealousy, lust and unclean thoughts. Wouldn't covetousness be behind these things in most cases? When we are critical, judgmental and jealous of others, we are coveting something or someone that somebody else has. We wish we had that same thing for ourselves. When we steal and kill and lust, we are doing what we have to in order to get what we want, at all costs. When we rebel, we are really envious down deep of that person, and when we gossip, we are really doing so because down deep there is a hidden jealousy factor.

"From whence come wars and fightings among you? Come they not hence, even of your lusts that war in your members? Ye lust, and have not: ye kill, and desire to have, and cannot obtain: ye fight and war, yet ye have not, because ye ask not. Ye ask, and receive not, because ye ask amiss, that ye may consume it upon your lusts. Ye adulterers and adulteresses, know ye not that the friendship of the world is enmity with God? whosoever therefore will be a friend of the world is the enemy of God. Do ye think that the Scripture saith in vain, The spirit that dwelleth in us lusteth to envy?" (James 4:1-5).

"Being filled with all unrighteousness, fornication, wickedness, covetousness, maliciousness, full of envy, murder, debate, deceit, malignity; whisperers, Back-biters, haters of God, despiteful, proud, boasters, inventors of evil things disobedient to parents, Without understanding, covenantbreakers, without natural affection, implacable, unmerciful: Who knowing the judgment of God, that they which commit such things are worthy of death, not only do the same, but have pleasure in them that do them" (Romans 1:29-32). Take a close look, envy is listed right next to murder! Sounds like it's something we are not to take lightly.

Idolatry

"Therefore say unto the house of Israel, Thus saith the Lord God; Repent, and turn yourselves from your idols; and turn away your faces from all your abominations. For every one of the house of Israel, or of the stranger that sojourneth in Israel, which separateth himself from me, and setteth up his idols in his heart, and putteth the stumblingblock of his iniquity before his face, and cometh to a prophet to inquire of him concerning me; I the Lord will answer him by myself: and I will set my face against that man, and will make him a sign and a proverb, and I will cut him off from the midst of my people; and ye shall know that I am the Lord" (Ezekiel 14:6-8).

Last, but not least, let's take a look at the sin of idolatry. Idolatry takes place anytime that something or someone comes between you and God and begins to take the place of time, money and energy that rightfully belongs to God. That person's heart becomes distant to the things of God as other things have crept in. He now fails to love the Lord with all of his heart, soul and mind.

Idolatry is a reflection of a problem from within. It is stemming from the hidden things in the heart and eventually shows up symptomatically in other body parts or places.

It can show up in people who we once thought were strong people in the Lord. It can show up in the form of what we would consider good things. Yes, good things such as church activities can become an idol if they take the place of a relationship with God. We can't get caught up in serving the work of the Lord instead of the Lord of the work.

Remember the story about Martha and Mary. Who did Jesus delight in? The one who was sitting at his feet, spending time with Him. We can become so busy serving in the Church and so easily forget all about the One who we serve.

Look at some of the people who were once in the Church serving the Lord with all of their heart. Now they are nowhere to be found. Maybe they fell to some of the horrible sins, such as adultery or alcoholism, but chances are they've fallen into the trap of idolatry.

Idols creep into our lives so easily. Our American lifestyles offer so much. Television and hobbies can become idols. Maybe they started out as a good thing, but now have taken the place of God in our lives. Our career can become an idol. Maybe it was once given to us supernaturally as a result of answered prayer, but now we have made it number one in our lives.

Habitually working on Sunday can be an idol. It's so hard to totally avoid shopping or working on Sunday in today's day and age, but when we prefer to work to get as much extra cash as we can over being in the House of God, we've made an idol.

Sometimes, this Christian walk can seem overwhelming. In our own strength, we could never attain it. Take heart, my friend, God has made a way.

Chapter 12 will reflect on God's saving power through the Blood. His grace is greater than any struggle I face. God would not give us any command that He had not given us the ability to be able to attain.

"This is the covenant that I will make with them after those days, saith the Lord, I will put my laws into their hearts, and in their minds will I write them; And their sins and iniquities will I remember no more" (Hebrews 10:16,17).

7

Here Comes the Judge!

"For with what judgement ye judge, ye shall be judged: and with what measure ye mete, it shall be measured to you again" (Matthew 7:2).

*O*ur world is filled with trials and problems. We would like to believe that we are immune from this world's cares and never fall prey to them, but unfortunately, that is not the case. We, ourselves are vulnerable to the snares of the devil and to our own shortcomings. We are a weak and unstable people. We cannot undo the mistakes that we have made in our lives. We can only make the best of things.

We go through life doing our best, trying to keep above the cares of this world, but inevitably, sooner or later, we are still bound to fall flat on our face. It takes true humility to reach the point where we admit, we've blown it and we need help. This is the first and hardest step. Then, we need to repent and seek God's forgiveness and rest in His love and mercy. We need to ask for power to remain overcomers. We then need to spend a little or much time, depending on the intensity of our wrongdoing, restoring the damage our sin caused our immediate family.

Just about the time that we are rejoicing in our victory and God's magnificent grace, da da da dum... Here comes the judge!

The judge? Yeah, the critical coworker, the nagging family member and, more often than not, a judgmental church member. They'll come to tell you what you could have told them years ago, you're not perfect! They seem to come faster than the devil himself.

We are called to be builder-uppers, not tearer-downers. We are called only to tear down Satan's works. We are so busy worrying about ourselves, we don't find out other's intentions or motives, and we jump to our own conclusions.

Never say it could never happen to you. You just might find yourself doing the same thing. I believe this often happens because we've meditated so much on what the other person has done wrong. It then enters our own mind, and before long, we find ourselves pondering on thoughts of the same wickedness.

God often brings things into our lives as a result of our judging other people. The Scriptures say that, "With what judgment we judge, we shall be judged" (Matthew 7:2). We're now back to the sowing and reaping process. We can't rebuke the harvest. We became critical, and now God is bringing circumstances into our own lives to help us to understand that, apart from His grace, we would have fallen too.

We cannot put our convictions from God on other people. Sure, some things are written in black and white in the Word of God that *Thou shalt not do it*!! No one can commit adultery, kill or steal and think that God will overlook it without true repentance. That's what the bulk of my book is dealing with.

There are some issues, however, that God deals with on an individual level that are not in black and white.

We must take into consideration that not everyone has been saved for the same amount of time; not everyone is in the same denomination; not everyone has been given the same amount of talents and expectations.

For example, maybe Mrs. A is 30 pounds overweight, and God is saying, "I am displeased." Whereas, Mrs. B, who lives across the street, is also 30 pounds overweight.

The Lord hasn't seen it fit to convict her of the same thing. Why? Probably because Mrs. A is overweight because she occupies her time in front of the television set with a bag of chips and 2 pieces of cake and 16 ounces of soda. The Lord has been pleading with her to spend time with Him in the Word, and she continues to put Him at the bottom of her list. She knows what she needs to do but has a lot of trouble getting up the willpower to do it.

Mrs. B, on the other hand, serves the Lord with all of her heart. She is a large-framed person by nature. She's had a few health reasons why she can't lose weight. Maybe the medicine she takes is known for causing weight gain. There is a drastic difference in the two scenarios, and God deals accordingly.

So often when we achieve victory in a certain area, we lack the patience that our friends need to attain victory in that same area. Maybe we had a real victory in an area that we struggled in for years. We are in jubilee over our exciting victory. We then go to church the next Sunday and *ewww*, Sally comes up to you to share some juicy gossip about Nellie, and you get mad at Sally for her immaturity. Have you forgotten that you just got victory in the same area yourself? Look how long it took you to get there!

I once witnessed a conversation where a girl was so disgusted with another girl because she couldn't give her hang-ups to the Lord. At first, I thought she had a legitimate gripe, as the other girl did come across as a whiney person. But then she went on to say, "All that she has to do is give it to God. I went to the altar last week and gave this same area to the Lord myself, and that is what she needs to do!"

I then realized there was something wrong with this picture. She was being insensitive to the fact that at her own admission she had *just* gotten the victory in this same area herself. Now, in turn, she was passing judgment on someone else to get on with it!

I believe the reason we tend to do this is that it puts a mirror in our face of what we were like for so long and reminds us of how ugly that behavior was. We are so excited about the "new me" that we want everyone to have it. We become critical of others who have the same struggles, when we would be a very effective source of help to them if we only had the love and patience.

One New Year's Eve I made a resolution to be five minutes early instead of five minutes late everywhere I went. I was successful at this commitment (for a few weeks anyway). All of a sudden, all of the chronic late people in my life became so annoying. What an awful habit it was to be tardy when looking at it from the other end of the coin.

I did this exact thing when I went on a well-balanced diet and lost a few pounds a few years back. After cutting back on my food intake many times, I was still unsuccessful in shedding those few extra pounds I had put on over the years. I finally found a proper diet plan that taught you that to lose weight the quickest and healthiest way was not only to avoid the wrong foods but to eat lots of the right foods. The more of the right foods that you eat, the more you would lose. I tried it, and it worked for me.

I lost six pounds the first week and two pounds the following, ending with a ten pound weight loss at the end of four weeks. Being short, these few pounds made a big difference. It looked like I dropped two sizes in one week. Though I only lost six pounds, I shed a total of two and a half inches, along with a lot of fluid I had been carrying. Low and behold, by the end of the first week, everybody else started to look so chubby! I went to the park, and there suddenly wasn't a thin person there. Just one week earlier, the same group of people all looked so good compared to me. I felt disgusted that they couldn't give up a few sweets to lose those couple of pounds that would make such a difference! I passed my convictions right down the line.

Dangers Of Comparing

Comparing is something that can produce great benefits or risks, mostly risks. Comparing yourself to the next person can bring encouragement or discouragement to your ego. Overall, it is a very unhealthy practice. Sometimes it can encourage you when you feel that you are the only person in the world with this great big problem. You might realize that there is always someone worse off than yourself. This could bring you some encouragement in a healthy way, as long as you don't become prideful in the process of it all. It could teach you a very valuable lesson.

More times than not, comparing brings very dangerous, ungodly results. It is a very uneasy feeling when
someone becomes judgmental of you. It is an extremely
uncomfortable position to be in that puts just as much
pressure on you as what it does on the guilty person. I
have, however, watched in situations where I was unjust-
ly criticized and saw how God worked to bring chastisement into the guilty party's life. I've watched God pour
out His blessings greatly upon me in the months to come,
while judgment was great upon my critic.

There have been many times, however, that I have
had to humble myself and say, "Okay, God, I am being
critical, and I need to look for the best in people. Please
help me not to be bitter toward them."

We cannot change others. No matter how hard we
try, we will never change our spouse, our coworker or
our brother in the Lord by pointing out their errors. We
need to lift one another up in prayer instead of trying to
change or manipulate each other to change. Manipula-
tion will only make them more rebellious, and it will
become more difficult to arrive at any solution. Let go,
and let God. Put them in His hands and watch the difference it will make.

Recently, we had occasion to switch churches *and*
denominations. We knew that God's divine guidance
was involved, but still, it was a big step. I had to put my
faith in action and let go and let God make the change
in everyone involved.

Being that we are a family of five, we did not expect
the transition to go 100 percent smoothly, so we took it
very slowly and allowed months for all the proper
adjustments to take place. There were five of us that

needed to let go of old friends and the things we were accustomed to doing, and five of us that needed to make new relationships. There were five of us that needed to be able to adjust to the new worship style and sermon style. There were five of us that needed to have adequate small group ministry provided. We all adjusted very well to the new change.

That is, everyone except for our middle child. She was just past her 13th birthday and was not at the point in her life that such an adjustment would come smoothly. When she realized that this really was going to be a sure thing, she got very emotionally upset. She cried a lot, withdrew a lot and wouldn't speak to us. We thought that it would be a very temporary thing and continued to follow through with the change that was taking place in our lives.

Things did not improve, however. In fact, they seemed to be getting worse. She was really attached to her friends and the style of our former church. We dealt with her with gentleness and patience and full understanding of what she was going through. We provided numerous opportunities for her to fellowship with her friends and let go slowly.

After about five months, however, we felt it was time to break away. Hoping that she would have accepted the fact by now, we entered her bedroom one weekend to announce our decision. Amber, age 13 at the time, was lying in bed with a severe eye infection. She was already kind of gloomy and not her usual cheery self anyway. The timing wasn't the greatest; the news immediately sent her into a strong emotional outburst of tears, and it was obvious to me that she was becoming depressed.

Her other four family members, on the other hand, were overjoyed with not only the fresh start they were experiencing, but also the fact that our new church was very rooted in the preaching and teaching of the Word. It also provided the incredible worship services, love and fellowship we all needed. The opportunities to both grow and serve were endless. They had the same vision for outreach that the Lord had been preparing our hearts for.

We needed the Lord's favor in dealing with our young teenager. That particular weekend, she had to stay home from church because of the contagious nature of her eye infection. We went to Sunday morning worship, relieved that we didn't have a teary-eyed teen beside us again this Sunday. It was becoming embarrassing. Down deep, however, my heart was crushed. I really wanted to see her start to blend in and get involved. I wanted to see her happy. I knew that the Lord had great things in store for her also.

I went back to the evangelistic service that Sunday evening. I knew it was time for a breakthrough in our circumstances. At altar service, I stood up front and really gave the situation to the Lord. I cried, "Lord, there is no doubt that You have lead us in this direction. Four of the five of us have adjusted extremely well. I cannot do anything or say anything to change our daughter's mind. It has to come with time. Since You have undoubtedly lead us here, I know You will provide the grace that is needed to make the rest of the transition smooth. You would not have moved in our lives the way that You did without providing a way." I left my burden there, at the altar, totally in the hands of the Lord.

From the moment we walked in the door of our home that evening, we knew that a supernatural work had taken place. Our daughter was no longer so withdrawn like she had been for months. She actually spoke to us! The next day we could hardly recognize that she was the same person. She talked our ears off.

The following day, we spent the evening with a family in the new church who had a daughter her age. I could hardly get over the radiance that was evident on Amber's face. She was a new creature. A change had taken place supernaturally. Nothing that we said or did made the difference. God intervened in the spiritual realm when I laid my burden at His feet, trusting Him for a solution. Where He guides, He truly provides.

I could not change my daughter's mind. It was something that needed to take place over a process of time and with some supernatural intervention. Only God, in the right timing can deal with some situations that we tend to want to resolve ourselves.

We cannot compare our circumstances with one another's. There is no way humanly possible, two people's circumstances will ever be totally alike. Comparing will eventually destroy us, body, soul and spirit.

So many times comparing ourselves to others gives us an inferiority complex. During my younger adult years, every time my house was at its messiest, I would remember the cleanest house I had ever been in and imagine that that housewife was standing in my home inspecting and criticizing every nook and cranny of my filthy house. When we have a habit of comparing ourselves to others, we are always going to come out short, because we'll always find someone who has it better than us. It only brings discouragement into our lives.

When we come to the point in our lives where we accept things that we cannot change, that is when God often moves and changes our circumstances. Early in our marriage, I dreamed for the day to come when I would get a house. Surely I deserved one. I had two young children and loved being a homemaker. Other moms were never at home, why did they deserve such nice houses?

When I came to the point in my life that I could truly say, "However long it takes to get a house, I *can* wait," I had a brand new house within the year. When we are able to let go of our dreams that we feel we just have to reach right now, they come back to us – provided they were meant to be. It's at the point we stop worrying about it and struggling so hard to get it, that things often fall into place. And when the Lord is in it, it usually happens quickly and smoothly when the right timing comes.

When we find ourselves jealous of a certain talent someone else has, we need to remember that it might be their natural, God-given ability. Just as writing is to me so easy and natural, some people could not begin to write a book, an article or even a report. On the flip side, my mother is very talented with very fine detailed oil painting, something that I could not begin to have the patience for. She can draw and paint turkeys and deer without any problem. If I drew a buck it would look like an oval with a circle for its head and stick feet, tail and horns. One time, while playing "Pictionary," I was instructed to draw a pig, and I could not even remember what kind of tail they have, so it ended up with a bunny tail!

When we find ourselves critical of someone's ability, we might need to take into account that it just isn't "their thing," just as drawing certainly isn't my thing. They might not be cut out to do the job that, for some reason, they were pressured to do.

Why We Aren't Qualified to Make a Judgment Call

Why can't we judge others when we see them doing wrong? Besides, we learned in the first chapter about being able to discern by the fruits of people's labors. First of all, we need to remember that God is the only righteous judge. He is the only one who sees the full picture.

We certainly don't want to open ourselves up to the judgment of God on our lives. Nor do we want to go through the lesson of learning that it doesn't pay to criticize. We can't put our convictions on other people. It's not always what was done, but sometimes why they did it. Often, it's the motive that counts.

When we become guilty of putting judgment on other people, we usually forget to keep things in perspective. We forget that we usually don't know all of the facts. In fact, it is impossible for anybody but the person themselves and God to know all of the facts. If we persist and continue to point the finger, God will allow something to come into our own life. We often bring judgment upon ourselves through our criticism of others. We need to recognize that if it wasn't for God's grace, we would have fallen too.

We need to remember when we are fast to draw our own conclusions that the person's situation may be drastically different than our own. They may be older or younger than you are. They may have been married longer or shorter than you have; they may have been in their profession longer or shorter than you; they may be more or less experienced than yourself in the matter. They may have been saved longer or shorter than you have been.

I don't care for the term *constructive criticism*. I prefer, if someone needs correction, using, "May I kindly suggest?" or "I thought of an idea that might be helpful for you." Criticism is criticism any way you cut it!

We need to keep our eyes on the Lord. If we do, we won't worry about what is going on around us. It helps us to keep focused even when things in lives get out of sorts. He is the one that they need to turn their situation over to, not you.

Maybe they have already repented of the sin. Maybe you are just now finding out about the problem. In fact, in most cases, when the big news comes out, whether good or bad, it's usually made known after the fact. Things don't just happen. It never ceases to amaze me how many times I hear people gullible enough to believe that things just happened.

I've heard some reactions from people who actually thought that so and so's marriage just fell apart all of a sudden. "Yeah, she just up and left him without any reason," they go on to tell me. No, things don't just happen! The facts leading to the end result build up over days, months and even years. Sometimes, they are a result of a series of events that have taken place over the lifetime of the party involved.

They never got to the root of the problem. They needed to identify the reoccurring source of contention and deal with it directly, breaking the reoccurring cycle of defeat.

Inability to deal with the root is a significant problem in our churches. Pews are filled with people who hold grudges and bitter feelings toward their parents, their siblings, their brother in the Lord, the minister and even God Himself. There is always an underlying problem involved. They need to get to the root of what is causing the reoccurring problems that just tend to go round in circles and round in circles – repent, seek forgiveness and go forth.

We don't know another's burdens. We must remember that people usually do things based on their emotions and their feelings. We react and then think, instead of think and then react. We don't know how much, how long they struggled first. We don't know how hard they tried to overcome the battle first. We, therefore, draw our own conclusions about people's reactions. Then we get our defenses up.

We need to be able to discern what is our own personal dealings between us and God and what is outright sin and dead wrong. For example, some people feel convicted that certain foods, such as meats, are wrong to eat. Other people believe God gave us animals for that reason. Whether you eat meat or are a vegetarian is not going to make the difference between heaven and hell.

We need to face the fact that we are part of the world. We live here and can't avoid all situations. We just can't participate in them the way the nonbeliever does. We need to refrain from as much as possible.

Many good parents want to avoid the issue of Santa Claus at all costs. When our first child was a toddler, we thought we might do the same. We soon resorted to telling him that Santa was just a fun character at Christmas, kind of like a cartoon character. He's a make-believe character who will give you an orange and a candy cane if you sit on his lap and tell him what you would really like to have this coming Christmas. He doesn't fly through the sky and come down your chimney, but he's a fictional character we can enjoy during our holiday planning. We never had a bit of trouble with any of our children as they got older with the issue of Santa Claus. They knew the truth from the beginning.

One of the most common times that we have a tendency to judge people is when we see their child misbehaving. We're almost always quick to conclude that the parents have made a negative impression on his or her life. Certainly, in many cases, this proves true. It's part of the sowing and reaping process. There are, however, so many more factors to consider in today's fast-paced world.

Society itself plays a heavy role on the behavior of our children. The modern technology of instant everything has trained this generation to be impatient. If you want it, you've got it at the press of a button. We have microwaves, remote controls, videos and computers that possess the minds of our youth. The school systems have changed drastically. Even the elementary school grades change teachers and roommates each and every year – something unheard of just a few years ago.

Our fast-paced, ever changing world has had a humongous influence on our children. They never have time to make any new adjustments until life takes a turn in another direction. Teenage pregnancy and divorce rates are very high. Not all negative influence in the lives of our children is coming directly from the home. There are so many more factors to consider. We must not always be so quick to bring judgment on the parents of an ill-behaved child.

My husband and I have three children. They are at three different age brackets, being that they were born three and six years apart. I've spent a number of years being stretched between trying to meet the needs of a adventurous teenager and an extremely active preschooler, while not forgetting the easy going middle child. While one of them is constantly a handful, the other child living in the same house during the same time frame couldn't be any more compliant. She has a totally different personality and a totally different out-look on life.

All three of our children are so unique in their tem-peraments. The oldest child is a very ambitious person. He talked (and argued) in paragraphs by the time he was a toddler. As a matter of fact, he still does at 17 years of age! He was always a very excitable person, even during his toddler years.

My second baby was a born crier. While pregnant with her, I heard that however active the baby was while carrying it was an indication of how it would be once it was born. I got concerned during my third trimester as she kicked constantly. There was move-ment all day and all night until about 5:00 a.m., then she would settle until about mid-morning when she began her active day again.

Sure enough, I gave birth to a baby that basically just cat-napped during the day, cried all night, then slept sound from 5:00 to 9:00 a.m. After she passed the trying toddler years, however, she developed into a very sweet, compliant personality that could brighten anyone's day. As a matter of fact, her nickname is Smiley.

Then came baby number three, and life has never been the same since. In addition to her endless amounts of energy, there are other factors involved. The same year that our oldest started high school, our middle child started middle school and the youngest child started elementary school! During her younger years, my average week was one of pure exhaustion and burnout.

It was interesting during the preschool years of her life to hear the comments that came in from the outside. The conclusions that people drew about my life were unbelievable! It is impossible to know all of the facts involved in someone's situation. Little did the people on the outside looking in know the burden I was really carrying. Little did they know what the real problem was.

Remember when the devil tried to tempt Jesus. He did so when He was fatigued and hungry. His most effective tool is to first drag down our physical bodies, which carries into the mental, then into the spiritual. Then he knows he can have a hay day with us.

The Hidden Motive

Most of the time, when judgment is placed on someone, there is a hidden jealousy factor involved. Stop and think about it. If you are honest with yourself, when you nit pick at another person, aren't you really, down deep, a little envious of them? We seldom are critical of those who we feel no competition with, but rather with those we see as our competitors; we bring judgment upon them in a flash.

Therefore, when other people attack you, criticize you and judge you, you can take comfort in knowing that there is probably just a jealousy factor involved. You may find yourself at wit's end wondering what you've done that is so bad. It's probably not what you are not, but what you are – the zeal you have for the Lord, the position that you hold or the talents that you possess – that is causing the other party to behave in such a manner. They have probably become envious of you. So when you are persecuted for righteousness sake, rejoice in knowing that the truth of the matter is that you are probably making a good impression in their lives, and they just aren't at the same maturity level that you are in the Lord to be able to handle it. The ultimate end most always brings out some hidden jealousy factor.

8

The Spirit/Flesh Battle

"For the flesh lusteth against the Spirit, and the Spirit against the flesh: and these are contrary the one to the other: so that ye cannot do the things that ye would" (Galatians 5:17).

Paul is my very favorite Bible character. He reveals such Godly wisdom in his writings yet displays humility before God and man. I thrive on some of the Scriptures written by Paul in the books of the New Testament. He is so honest and down to earth. He reveals his continual struggle in wanting to do right, yet always battling inwardly with the flesh.

In both I Corinthians 15:9 and Ephesians 3:8, He refers to himself as the least of the apostles. He's not the least of my heroes. His in depth insight into the principles of life are just an incredible influence on my life.

Listen to the intense struggle described in Romans 7:14-24: "For we know that the law is spiritual: but I am carnal, sold under sin. For that which I do I allow not: for what I would, that do I not; but what I hate, that do I. If then I do that which I would not, I consent unto the law that it is good. Now then it is no more I that do it, but sin that dwelleth in me. For I know that in me (that is, in my flesh,) dwelleth no good thing: for to will is present with me; but *how* to perform that which is good I find not. For the good that I would I do not: but the evil which I would not, that I do. Now if I do that I would not, it is no more I that do it, but sin that dwelleth in me. I find then a law, that, when I would do good, evil is present with me. For I delight in the law of God after the inward man: But I see another law in my members, warring against the law of my mind, and bringing me into captivity to the law of sin which is in my members. O wretched man that I am! Who shall deliver me from the body of this death?"

Doesn't it seem so familiar? No matter how hard we try, it seems that we just can't ever attain what we picture to be God's perfect Will for our level of Christian maturity. We say, starting today we are going to do it. We are going to go the highest in the things of God. Nothing will stifle our zeal for the Lord. Then, *bam!* A day later, we find ourselves laying flat on our face in a mud puddle. What went wrong? We were so sincere.

A few years back, I remember very vividly making a commitment. I had heard that if you do something for 21 days straight it becomes a habit, good or bad. So I decided to really seek the ultimate level of holiness. I said that for the month of May I would not allow anything negative to come out of my mouth. I would not say anything bad about anything or anybody. This was at a point in my life when I felt strong enough and mature enough in the Lord that I could certainly attain such a strong commitment.

Wow, the devil must have known what glory God would have gotten if I had accomplished success! By the second day, I thought I was going to go crazy, the spiritual warfare seemed so intense. By the third day, I had become angry with God and outright irate, drawing the conclusion, after serving the Lord all of my life, that it was an impossible thing to be able to do.

If I remember correctly, I purposely broke the goal during the first week, hoping that satan would buzz off. I got on the phone to chat about another person, knowing full well what I was doing. I developed an "I don't care" attitude. I felt I could not live this Christian life any longer; it was much too difficult. I turned totally rebellious toward the grace of God. The spiritual warfare was great.

Within six weeks, this horror story turned into victory. As I gave my anger to the Lord, He was not only gracious enough to forgive, but He took the whole situation and turned it around for my good!

There are certainly times in all of our lives when we can identify with the Apostle Paul's struggle to avoid doing the things he knew full well he was not permitted to be involved in. We all struggle with temptation; no one is immune to falling prey to the devil's devices.

"*This* I say then, Walk in the Spirit, and ye shall not fulfil the lust of the flesh. For the flesh lusteth against the Spirit, and the Spirit against the flesh: and these are contrary the one to the other: so that ye cannot do the things that ye would" (Galatians 5:16,17).

We need to remember that we were all once lost in our sins. Apart from a salvation experience, not one of us will make it. When we were still in the world, we did the same things as those who are still lost.

"And you hath he quickened, who were dead in trespasses and sins; Wherein in time past ye walked according to the course of this world, according to the prince of the power of the air, the spirit that now worketh in the children of disobedience: Among whom also we all had our conversation in times past in the lusts of our flesh, fulfilling the desires of the flesh and of the mind; and were by nature the children of wrath, even as others. **But God...** who is rich in mercy, for his great love wherewith he loved us, Even when we were dead in sins, hath quickened us together with Christ (by grace ye are saved;)" (Ephesians 2:1-5).

II Corinthians 5:17 certainly baffles a lot of good people. If we are new creatures according to this verse, why do we struggle so within ourselves to do what is right. The desire certainly is there, the willingness and want to, but it often seems like we continually find ourselves reverting to the temptation to want to allow a little of the old flesh to creep back in. Why does the flesh always seem to get in the way of our desire for holiness?

We can't expect to obtain the ultimate level of holiness overnight. It is an ongoing process of cleansing and growing. Let's face it, seldom does a person come to Christ as a brand new Christian and give up, overnight, every sinful habit they have ever had. There should be a drastic immediate change, but it's a working out of our salvation that comes from a day by day walk with the Lord.

It's like continually having to pull the weeds out of our flower bed. It's an ongoing task. Kind of like cleaning house. It only stays spick and span for a short while, then we start all over again. But, the less we let it get out of order as we go along, the easier it is to shine it up the next time.

Ever prepared for a yard sale? You go through your home and find some junk that you will gladly part with.

Then you come to some appliances that you just don't find yourself using. You decide to do the right thing and part with it, but when you go to price it, you find that you just can't get near the value that it had not too long ago when you bought it new.

As things grow old quickly, so does our spiritual walk if we don't continually keep it fresh and new. We need to shine it up on a daily basis. We are vulnerable people; our flesh is weak.

"Watch ye and pray, lest ye enter into temptation. The spirit truly is ready, but the flesh is weak" (Mark 14:38).

Often the best weapon against the flesh battle is simple avoidance. Watch a parent of a toddler in the 18 to 24-month-old age range. Some parents leave their valuables out in the path of the tot and do well teaching them "hands off." Others find it an endless battle with the strong-willed little determined one. They often end up giving up the battle and moving temptation out of the way, while some still attempt to teach the toddler what his boundaries are.

Sometimes, the best thing you can do as a Christian, if you continuously seem to struggle with the temptation to regress to the old nature, is simply to take the temptation out of the way. If you keep going into the stores and carrying those credit cards, sure, you are eventually going to hit a weak day. If you keep going to the club where the old partying gang hangs out, sure, you are eventually going to get the urge all over again. If you battled with fornication in your past and choose to watch an X-rated movie, you might just find yourself suffering a lot of temptation. It might be best to move temptation out of the way and stay clear of it to begin with!

"But put ye on the Lord Jesus Christ, and make not provision for the flesh, to fulfil the lusts thereof" (Romans 13:14).

Nothing Hid

Sometimes it seems like the wicked will always prevail and never get their reward. It seems like their contrary ways continue and they will get away with taking advantage of good people and living like the devil forever.

Many good Christian people are tormented by the unfairness this life has to offer. Many allow their wounds to fester to the point of bitterness. We need to remember, when we are hurt by the things that people do, that they are responsible for their actions. We cannot change the circumstance. However, if we dwell on our hurts and allow bitterness to creep in, then we become responsible for our response to their actions. Now, the negative results have multiplied. We now, not only need to be reconciled to our enemies, but we need to make our peace with God. We need to seek His forgiveness for allowing our emotions to get out of control and restore a right relationship both with God and mankind.

Be assured, my friend, though it seems like evil will prevail forever, God will some day put an end to it once and forever. He is the just judge of all sin and wrongdoing.

Sometimes, we do witness the devastation of the consequences of sin in those who have fallen. Have you ever witnessed the stages of those who have fallen to an adul-

terous affair? What a horrible sight is the end result
when they realize what they have done! The devil hid
the price tag, well... for a season. Then, the same evil one
who made things look so pleasurable at one time, turned
around and became the same evil one that uses that
which once was pleasurable to bring condemnation.

It is a traumatic picture to see when the consequences of sin catch up with a person, but in all honesty,
I would rather it catch up with them on this earth when
they have time to seek God's holy forgiveness, than to
stand before God and hear the words, "I never knew
you."

You have to wonder what people think when they go
through life without the fear of God rooted within their
beings. What makes them think they will get away with
their habitual sins? There are numerous Scripture pas-
sages forewarning us that our sins will find us out!

"For nothing is secret, that shall not be made manifest; neither any thing hid, that shall not be known and
come abroad" (Luke 8:17).

"Some men's sins are open beforehand, going before
to judgment; and some men they follow after" (I Timothy 5:24).

"Ye have sinned against the Lord: and be sure your
sin will find you out" (Numbers 32:23).

"For it is a shame even to speak of those things
which are done of them in secret. But all things that are
reproved are made manifest by the light: For whatsoever doth make manifest is light" (Ephesians 5:12,13).

"Neither is there any creature that is not manifest in
his sight: but all things are naked and opened unto the
eyes of him with whom we have to do" (Hebrews 4:13).

Sometimes we feel like people are like God; they notice every step we make and we could never get away with a simple little "white lie." My husband is often like that. We have a very honest, open relationship. We don't keep anything from one another; we share most everything with one another. He, however, has much higher convictions in the area of honesty than what I do, or what most people would.

I will never forget our first year of marriage. It was back when we had time to do everything together, including all of our grocery shopping. We came out of the grocery store one day, into the parking lot and loaded the car with our bags. As I was buckling into the passenger's seat, he looked over at me and said, "Do you want to take this back to the cashier, she overpaid me?" He then proceeded to hand me four cents!

Well, I looked at him and exclaimed, "Are you nuts!?! She'll laugh me to scorn; that's ridiculous! If you think you have to give it back, you go right in there and give it to her!"

He calmly, quietly got out of the car and proceeded to do so. I then sank down in my seat as if the whole world was watching what had taken place. Certainly, the cashier would think he was as silly as what I thought!

Now, 18 years later, I am slowly but surely learning to appreciate the honesty of my husband who lives up to his name. Frank, meaning honesty fits him through and through.

I've seen so many so-called Christian men throughout our marriage who, at their own admission, cheat on their taxes, work for under-the-table cash to avoid pay-

ing Uncle Sam and/or fail to report that extra cash to
the unemployment office. They habitually work on the
Lord's Day and fall for every get-rich quick scheme they
can find!

Some use God's name in vain, make hobbies their
idol and their jobs their god. Many treat their wives as
a punching bag and load them with the sole responsibility of child-raising.

I have finally come to grips with the fact that what
most of us would consider a little overboard in the area
of honesty, is actually a blessing. It says a lot for his
character. He is a family man with high morals and
Godly standards.

I thank God for the move of revival that I am witnessing in the lives of many of our Christian men across
the nation. Men are returning to Godly standards and
saying with assurance in their faith in God, "As for me
and my house, we will serve the Lord" (Joshua 24:15).

The All-knowing God

Did you ever go on vacation and notice all of the
thousands of people and wonder how can God keep
track of everyone. Think about it! God knows everything about everybody in every city, state, country,
nation and generation. It's mind boggling! I can't even
keep up with myself! Every person from Adam to the
last baby born in America, He knows inside out.

The good news is that He not only knows our shortcomings, but He also knows and sees every good deed
we've ever done! He cares about us with an everlasting
love. Even the hairs of our heads are numbered. We
truly serve an awesome God!

Warfare

Jesus himself knows what it is to be tempted by the devil. How could this happen? When did this happen? When He was very tired and hungry. What an opportune time for the devil to make his move. He had found the perfect timing, so he thought.

Fatigue is an excellent tool for the devil to use as he always waits until we hit a low point, and then he makes his attack. It is the open window he's been waiting for. We may be tired, hungry, down, not feeling well or simply having a bad day, and he will come knocking on the doors of your mind. You see, that's where he usually attacks first, in your mind, because that's where all wrong-doing begins.

Hurts are nursed in our minds. Miscommunication festers in our minds. Low self-esteem breeds in the mind. Tormenting fears develop in our minds. Depression is often a by-product of things that are triggered in the mind. I can attest time and time again of times when I have become fatigued, over-committed, burnt-out, and the enemy came in like a flood to trouble my mind. It was during these same times that I often experienced severe bouts of depression and even an occasional anxiety attack.

Surprisingly, it wasn't even at times of difficulty in my life. In fact, it was often when I was involved in good things, such as a two-week revival that kept me on the go or involvement in an Easter drama. Some people may be quick to say that the devil attacked me simply because he didn't want me involved in God's work. I agree, but the bigger factor was simply that I had exhausted my time and energy with continuously being overly busy, and the devil had an opportune time to play games with my mind.

He surely isn't going to tempt us when we have just returned from a refreshing vacation or a service where God sent an overdose of strength throughout our body, soul and spirit. He knows that we are spiritually built up and strong. He waits until we are having a bad-hair day and then... "He comes in as a roaring lion, seeking whom he may devour" (I Peter 5:8). That's why the verse starts out saying we must "be sober, vigilant" and verse nine goes on to say, "Whom resist stedfast in the faith."

There was never in all of history a more important time to be rooted in the Word of God and equipped for warfare, putting on the armor of God.

"Finally, my brethren, be strong in the Lord, and in the power of his might. Put on the whole armor of God, that ye may be able to stand against the wiles of the devil. For we wrestle not against flesh and blood, but against principalities, against powers, against the rulers of the darkness of this world, against spiritual wickedness in high places. Wherefore take unto you the whole armor of God, that ye may be able to withstand in the evil day, and having done all, to stand. Stand therefore, having your loins girt about with truth, and having on the breastplate of righteousness; And your feet shod with the preparation of the gospel of peace; Above all, taking the shield of faith, wherewith ye shall be able to quench all the fiery darts of the wicked. And take the helmet of salvation, and the sword of the Spirit, which is the word of God" (Ephesians 6:10-17).

Press On!

"For I reckon that the sufferings of this present time are not worthy to be compared with the glory which shall be revealed in us (Romans 8:18).

How plain the Scriptures spell it out that being a Christian does *not* assure you an easy life. In fact, it says quite the opposite. You should expect sufferings and persecutions.

"Beloved, think it not strange concerning the fiery trial which is to try you, as though some strange thing happened unto you: But rejoice, inasmuch as ye are partakers of Christ's sufferings; that, when his glory shall be revealed, ye may be glad also with exceeding joy" (I Peter 4:12,13).

"Yea, and all that will live godly in Christ Jesus *shall* suffer persecution" (II Timothy 3:12).

The saddest thing that I have witnessed over and over again in the Body of Christ today is that the greatest persecution, the greatest battles and the greatest amount of false accusations come from within the church itself. We could probably handle the persecution that we know we have to suffer if we are truly sold out for the sake of the gospel, if it would come from the world. If that was the case, we would expect it and understand it.

It never ceases to amaze me, however, that the bulk of the attacks nowadays come directly from other church members – usually from those who have lower standards than our own. It is downright devastating to see this problem sweeping through so many Christian groups and organizations today.

"For it was not an enemy that reproached me; then I could have borne it: neither was it he that hated me that did magnify himself against me; then I would have hid myself from him: But it was thou a man mine equal, my guide, and mine acquaintance. We took sweet counsel together, and walked unto the house of God in company" (Psalm 55:12-14). My, oh my. Read the next verse. "Let death seize upon them, and let them go down quick into hell: for wickedness is in their dwellings, and among them" (verse 15). How serious a matter of backbiting one another in the Church!

The Lord's army seems to be the only army that is so good at killing its own soldiers. What an opportunity for the devil to prevail! I bet he just has a hay day as he watches church people continuously warring against one another. Always having something critical to say, always sticking their noses where they don't belong, always jealous of the next person's talents and willingness to use their gifts for the glory of the furtherance of the Gospel.

We must use these seasons in our lives as opportunities to grow. If nothing else, persecution will surely teach you the art of perseverance. It is at these times in our lives that we can grow stronger and become more rooted in our Maker than ever before.

"But as for you, ye thought evil against me; but God meant it unto good, to bring to pass, as it is this day, to save much people alive" (Genesis 50:20).

When it seems like nothing good can come out of a situation, God is using the same situation to work in us something that He wants to develop. I can truly relate to Romans 5:3-5, which tells us that tribulations bring about good results if we allow them to make us and not break us: "But we glory in tribulations also: knowing that tribulation worketh patience; And patience, experience; and experience, hope; And hope maketh not ashamed; because the love of God is shed abroad in our hearts by the Holy Ghost which is given unto us."

I have learned some Godly wisdom through some tough experiences. In my younger years, I was always a very shy, introverted person who let people walk over me like a doormat. As a result, I took on the opposite traits in my young adult years. I turned that inward anger outward and became very defensive and outspoken. With the help of the Lord, I have learned to balance things out. First of all, I've learned never to respond to anyone when I'm very upset, but to wait until the heat of the moment is calmed down. Then, I can more adequately deal with things without bringing my emotions on the scene. Then, I need to make a wise decision of whether to confront the other person or simply pray for them. I have learned that some things are better when left unsaid. God will do a better job in dealing with people.

If you struggle with strong hurts from your past or present circumstances, trying something practical might help you through it. After seeking the Lord for forgiveness for any fault you might have in the matter, praying for the other party involved, confronting them if necessary, you may still struggle with some strong emotions if you were wronged.

Try this: Simply take a pencil and paper and write down your negative feelings. Name the person, the problem and what you think of them. It may not be pleasant, but God already knows what you are thinking anyway.

This should be a short procedure. Write out your angry words. Get it out of your system. Remember what is on the inside is going to come out in one form or another anyway. Then ball it up and throw it in the trash. Rejoice that you are no longer a servant to your hurt and go on with life. It's now behind you, even if the other party involved did not choose to make restitution.

One day, the Lord asked me a question that really changed my life, "Do you want to be remembered for carrying this burden around for the rest of your life?" Boy, did I ever change my actions fast! In the areas of my life that it was within my means to help myself, I got the victory, and in the areas that I could not seem help myself, I sought the expertise of someone who could help me.

At another time, I was wrestling with where the Lord had me at that stage in my life, and I had not totally accepted it. I opened up my feelings with a friend. She asked me a question that really made me stop and think! "Joy, have you really given this situation to the Lord?"

We go through life carrying burdens that we don't need to carry. God wanted me to keep my joy in that which He had lead me to do. I was taking what God had directed me to and trying to do it in my own strength. I am now learning to let God bring a healthy balance into that area of my life that was so out of order for so long. I now can rejoice in the great insight I've learned through the many painful experiences I had to go through in my life.

Your burdens are not worth carrying around. Take them to the altar and leave them there. Put them behind you. Our bodies were not made to handle the excessive baggage.

You see, sulking in our troubles does not change the fact. We have to come to the place where we can say point blank, "I *do* have this problem. I wish I did *not* have this problem, but I *do* have this problem. I wish I did *not* have this credit card maxed out, but I *do* have it maxed to the limit. I wish my child was *not* born with a handicap, but he *was* born with a handicap. I wish I did *not* lose my job, but I *did* lose my job. The fact is I *do* have this problem, so I *must* deal with it. I *must* take care of its roots so that it does not keep reoccurring."

This is a process that usually involves spiritual matters, mental matters and physical matters. All must be dealt with one by one, beginning with the spiritual. As we take care of it from that end, the others will be easier to handle.

In all of the stages of my Christian walk, I can honestly look back and say that this was the greatest time of growth I have ever experienced in my life! I stand in awe of what the Lord has developed in my life through all the high waters, Red Seas that He has walked me through. He did not take me out of it until He walked me through it.

Shortly after a long series of numerous trials and tribulations, I attended a ladies' ministry meeting. We were given a quiz that helped us to determined what our ministry gift was. There were seven categories. I scored very high in all seven. It was very difficult to narrow down which one was my natural God-given gift.

All seven areas I had excelled in after applying the great insights I learned through all the fiery trials that the Lord had delivered me from. It is in times of tribulation, that the Lord develops in us character that is used to raise us up to a higher level of ministry.

I have been blessed with many Christian leaders, ministers, friends and Bible studies throughout the course of my life, but no other was a greater teacher than learning the art of perseverance that came through the devastation of persecution!

"But we have this treasure in earthen vessels, that the excellency of the power may be of God, and not of us. We are troubled on every side, yet not distressed; we are perplexed, but not in despair; Persecuted, but not forsaken; cast down, but not destroyed; Always bearing about in the body the dying of the Lord Jesus, that the life also of Jesus might be made manifest in our body" (II Corinthians 4:7-10).

Never, when being falsely accused, throw your hands up and say, "I quit!" That's exactly what your enemies want you to do! If you give in, you are the defeated one. You have bent to their lower morales. So many people, when they get their feelings hurt or suffer ridicule from those around them, throw in the towel and say, "Well, I am not going back there! If that's what Christianity is, I don't need it!" They might as well wish the devil congratulations; that's exactly what he wanted to achieve. The best thing to do when you are knocked down, is to get right back up, put your chin up and go right back to doing what you know you were called to do.

If you have to say, "If that's Christianity, I don't need it," chances are you're right – they are not real

Christians. I believe it's possible that more people are going to hell as a result of watching so-called Christians backbiting and devouring one another, than from any other problem. That's why I am covering so much about the importance of holiness and checking out their fruits. True believers produce good fruits. Instead of turning away from the Lord as a result of someone else's poor witness, why don't you rejoice in the blessing of having learned the art of discernment in such a critical day and age?

Persevere, press on! The Lord will be your vengeance. He has a way of turning things around. Usually the rope that critics use on other's throats will come back to tie their own someday.

Be assured that if you are in right standing with God, He is on your side! It would be better if you suffer for the right in your life than for the wrong in your life. "But and if ye suffer for righteousness' sake, happy are ye: and be not afraid of their terror, neither be troubled; But sanctify the Lord God in your hearts: and be ready always to give an answer to every man that asketh you a reason of the hope that is in you with meekness and fear: Having a good conscience; that, whereas they speak evil of you, as of evildoers, they may be ashamed that falsely accuse your good conversation in Christ. For it is better, if the will of God be so, that ye suffer for well doing, than for evil doing. For Christ also hath once suffered for sins, the just for the unjust, that he might bring us to God, being put to death in the flesh, but quickened by the Spirit" (I Peter 3:14-18).

It is proper at times, once you've been through the fire and scorched by the flames, to pray that God will remove you from the arena of hurts. It may be necessary for your own well-being. It is healthier for you to be taken out of the constant reminders of the pain and placed in a healthier environment. Usually, when God pulls us through a painful situation, He places us in another atmosphere that tends to bring blessing in the same area that was once very painful to us.

"For our light affliction, which is but for a moment, worketh for us a far more exceeding and eternal weight of glory" (II Corinthians 4:17).

Following is a poem that I wrote on September 25, 1994 after hearing a sermon about the mountains in our life.

What Do You Do When The Mountain Doesn't Move?

What do you do when the mountain doesn't move?
When the sun doesn't shine
When God doesn't seem to come through?

What do you do when hope is all gone?
When despair is enlarged
And your spirit has grown worn?

Hold on dear child
Just keep pressing on
Cleave to your faith
And know someday you'll overcome.

Believe what they tell us: "This too shall pass"
This life is not our own
These earthen trials only serve to keep us on our knees
 And draw us near the throne.

For the sufferings of today
Can't compare to heaven's story
Those snags and struggles in this life
Develop you and bring Him glory.

Hard Headed or Hard Hearted?

Have you ever met a person so affected by hurts in their life that they've become cold to any type of help anyone has to offer? Some become so withdrawn you cannot reach them. Others become so outraged, you could never get the final word in. I have dealt with a lot of people that expect help and almost demand that you are in a position to be the one to help them. But, at any attempt that you put forth to help, they put up a wall and can't receive your love. They then become depressed and more withdrawn.

I've been there, done that. I've both done that to others and been on the receiving end of the frustration experienced when people look to you to be their savior. This is not a comfortable position to find yourself in and, to the best of your ability, should be avoided.

Dependency on other people is a very dangerous position to be in. We need to put our faith and trust in God and God alone. He is the only one who will never let us down. People who are in a position of ministry to others, often have people flocking to them like they are a star or a hero or even God Himself. Some people are so desperately looking for help anywhere they can find it that when they find someone who is willing to help, they smother them for attention to the point that they end up pushing away a person who could have provided the very source of help that they needed.

These people often try to develop new relationships, but seem to have extremely high expectations of those they look up to. They lean on them like they have been very close friends for a long time. What they fail to realize is that friendships take much time and effort to develop.

The Lord showed me one day that our relationship with Him is the same way. There are great benefits in serving the Lord, but we must realize that He wants us to develop a strong relationship with Him first. Then, He will start giving of Himself to us. It is at this point that He often chooses to heal our bodies, deliver us from bondage and meet our material needs.

What we often classify as anger toward man, really turns out to be anger toward God when we examine our hearts. Think about it. Think of something that tends to really gripe you. Are you really mad at your neighbor, or down deep, are you really feeling angry with God that your neighbor appears to be more blessed than you. You are living a more upright life than he is, but he seems to be problem free, and blessings seem to consistently flow his way. If not dealt with, our bitterness will turn to hardening of our hearts.

I used to have a real pet peeve with people who had good paying jobs and wasted their money so carelessly. My family was a good steward of every dollar that came in but continuously struggled to make ends meet. After years of judging people who neglected to be budget conscious, I finally came to realize that my anger was really toward God. Why didn't He allow us faithful stewards to have a comfortable living? It took me many years of marriage to stop comparing my situation to other families. I had to deal with my resentfulness.

We need to take seriously the warnings against hardening our heart toward the things of God. We must be softened enough to let the Holy Spirit work through us and in us what He wants to do in our lives.

God Turns Them Over

"Hear, O earth: behold, I will bring evil upon this people, even the fruit of their thoughts, because they have not hearkened unto my words, nor to my law but rejected it" (Jeremiah 6:19).

So what can happen when a man hardens his heart toward God? What happens when the root of bitterness continues to fester and grow and a blockage develops between man and God?

"Because that, when they knew God, they glorified *him* not as God, neither were thankful; but became vain in their imaginations, and their foolish heart was darkened. Professing themselves to be wise, they became fools, And changed the glory of the incorruptible God into an image made like to corruptible man, and to birds, and four-footed beasts, and creeping things. Wherefore **God also gave them up** to uncleanness through the lusts of their own hearts, to dishonour their own bodies between themselves: Who changed the truth of God into a lie, and worshipped and served the creature more than the Creator, who is blessed for ever. Amen. For this cause **God gave them up** unto vile affections: for even their women did change the natural use into that which is against nature: And likewise also the men, leaving the natural use of the woman, burned in their lust one toward another; men with men working that which is unseemly and receiving in themselves that recompense of their error which was meet. And even as they did not like to retain God in *their* knowledge, **God gave them over** to a reprobate mind, to do those things which are not convenient; Being filled with all unrighteousness, fornication, wickedness, covetousness, maliciousness; full of envy, murder, debate, deceit, malignity; whisperers, Backbiters, haters of God, despiteful, proud, boasters, inventors of evil things, disobedient to parents, Without understand, covenantbreakers, without natural affection, implacable, unmerciful: Who knowing the judgment of God, that they which commit such things are worthy of death, not only do the same, but have pleasure in them that do them" (Romans 1:21-32).

God clearly warns us that His spirit will not always strive with man. If we continue to refuse to choose to heed His call, He may just turn us over, give us up to our unclean desires. He is a gentleman, He will not push His way into our lives if we don't care for Him to be there.

If there seems to be a breakthrough in an area of frustration, we must ask ourselves, "Has it resulted because we've handed the controls over to God, or has God handed the controls over to us?" When we refuse to submit our will to God's, this Scripture passage clearly warns us that God will turn us over to our own desires. He often gives us the desires of our heart in a way that is not pleasant. When we persist in getting our own way, eventually He gives it to us. He then allows us to pay the consequences of our own choosing.

Sometimes, our circumstances get pretty heavy before we finally surrender our will to God's Will. If we allow these times in our lives to make us better and not bitter, God will teach us great and powerful things. It's so much easier when we give up the battle and hand over the controls. Let go and let God!

9

But... God!

*"And we know that all things work together for
the good to them that love God, to them who
are the called according to his purpose"*
(Romans 8:28).

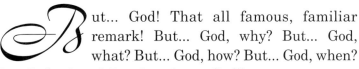ut... God! That all famous, familiar remark! But... God, why? But... God, what? But... God, how? But... God, when? But God, where? But, but, but... God!!

If we were to peak into God's big diary, probably the question that we would find asked by people most often is, "Why God? I just don't understand, why?"

Why did I miscarriage the pregnancy I waited so long for, when millions of babies are being aborted? Why did I give birth to six girls in eight years, when we wanted a boy so badly? Why did my wife leave me; I've been so faithful to her? Why did my neighbor's child get killed by a drunk driver? Why was my cousin's baby born with Downs Syndrome? Why did the transmission go out at the worst possible time? Why did a tornado destroy everything we ever owned? Why did my parent's home burn down and everything was lost including photos of my childhood memories? Why did the most faithful servant in my church suffer a severe heart attack? Why did my husband lose his job? Why did my minister resign? Why did my favorite evangelist fall to adultery? Why did a man on the news freak out and kill ten human beings?

Our world is full of unfairness. Hurt and wounded people are everywhere. We live in a very cruel world, and sometimes, we turn our anger and resentfulness toward God. If God were really God, how could He let me be suffering like this? Why doesn't *He* do something to stop pain and suffering?

God didn't promise us that life would always be a rose garden. It rains on the just and the unjust. Many of the heroes of the Bible went through traumatic experiences. Look at Job and all of the continuous difficulties he had to go through. Most of us would have a bad case of the woes after any one of his many tragedies.

Maybe it would help if we could realize that the theory that Christianity will always be a bed of roses is one big myth. We hear a lot of false teaching nowadays that it is God's Will for everyone to be prosperous, always healed the first time we pray, always a banging success at everything they attempt. Not many of us are so perfect that we could be taken out of this world like the Prophet Enoch. Most of us have to wait for the day the Lord delivers us out of this old world of sin and sorrow through death or the rapture.

"Precious in the sight of the Lord is the death of his saints" (Psalms 116:15).

When someone who is a Christian has an intense fear of death, you have to wonder what is really bothering them? Certainly, none of us feel totally comfortable with the issue, but we can have a peace that passeth all understanding. I, myself, in my mid-twenties and then again in my early thirties came face to face with a life-threatening situation. Though, I can admit to some feelings of trauma and terror, I can also remember a peace that it was well with my soul.

When I had emergency gallbladder surgery in 1990, I was told that it was so critical that if the surgeon waited another few hours there was a chance that they might lose me because it was at the stage that infection was ready to set into the blood stream. I had a feeling of sadness, of course, as you never know what might happen when faced with your first major operation.

I can attest, however, that in the emergency room, an overwhelming peace was present as I acknowledged to the Lord that whatever He chose to do was in His control. There was nothing that I could do to change the circumstance. He would have to take care of my family if He chose to take my life at just 27 years of age. It had to have been a supernatural strength; I was always a person who could not let God have the controls of my life. I took comfort in knowing that my life was lived in the fear of the Lord and it was well with my soul.

We need to realize that it is society that puts these unrealistic expectations on life as a Christian, and it was never recorded in the Word of God that this would be the case.

But God What?

But... God, what are you doing? We've all had this thought cross our mind. I thought God was leading me in this direction, and all of a sudden, things seem to be going in that direction. What do you think you're doing, God?

I've often witnessed this scenario. When there was a problem, things were prayed through, a good report came back, and just about the time the shouting hallelujah party began, the situation took a complete turn for the worse.

Sometimes, it seems like bad news turns to the good and then reverts to worse again. Earlier in our marriage, my husband was laid off. It was so difficult in starting over again to find a job that was not shift work. Being young and limited in job options, the only thing available seemed to be night shift, which would be hard on our family with a toddler and a baby.

Then one day it happened! A job near home, Monday through Friday from 8:00 a.m. to 4:30 p.m.! We were literally jumping up and down in our living room.

Well, at the end of the first day, my husband brought home the disappointing news that it wasn't what he expected. The next night he came home a nervous wreck and called his new boss up and quit.

I wanted to crawl in a hole. I had called different people who had prayed with us for a day job to testify of the great news. Now the good news had turned upside down.

In time, things did work out. At his most recent company banquet, he received a gold pin for his ten year award, of which the entire time was day shift. In fact, there are no evening positions in the company. His employment is local, and it provides health insurance for our family. God is faithful.

But... God, How?

Another commonly asked question! How, just how is God gonna do it? He said He will meet my needs. He said He would provide. He said He will answer our prayers, but how does He plan on doing it?

This also is a question that often baffles me. I am a person who always has to analyze things, always needing the game plan presented to me before I say, "I do." I need to know exactly what I am getting involved in, what's going to take place, how it's going to happen. I don't appreciate surprises. Not even nice surprises.

Generally speaking, my husband can save his money on a surprise bouquet of flowers on those special occasions. I prefer planned dates and gifts or balloons. I never was too bothered about flowers that would die and wither in a few days.

By the time we reached our 15-year wedding anniversary, I realized how unusual it was to never expect or receive a floral arrangement for your big day. It was starting to get embarrassing when friends would ask, "What did Joy get for Valentine's Day?" So, I started throwing out the hint. I bought my husband a dozen solid chocolate roses for Valentine's and told him he couldn't eat them until he gave me my first dozen roses.

Six weeks later, I went to work and headed straight for the transcription room where I occasionally would help with typing. When I walked in, a coworker said, "Happy Anniversary, I like your flowers."

"Uh, what flowers? Did my husband send flowers here? I didn't notice them yet." The big day finally arrived, and I sat at a different desk than what I normally did! Nevertheless, people that know me well don't throw too many surprises my way. They know my system can't handle too many unplanned events!

When I feel God is leading an area of my life in another direction, I find myself saying, "Okay God, but I want all of the details spelled out first." Why? What?

How? When? And Where? He's been a gentleman, He hasn't ever totally overwhelmed me or given me too much to handle. I am slowly but surely learning to trust Him. The more I let go and let God, the easier it becomes!

Think about it. Asking God, "How?" is really displaying a lack of faith in His divine wisdom. His thoughts and His ways are so much higher than ours. He doesn't always tell us how He's going to do it, but *if* He says He will, He will.

But... God, When?

When, when, when, when when? I want it now! This comment also exposes my impatient nature. I've always been an extremely impatient person. When I make up my mind to do something, I am one who will get it done at all costs. I might lose sleep, and there might not be any clean socks in the house in the process of it all, but I will achieve! Not everyone else is on the same pace, so I might run over a few people that get in my way. I don't have much patience with people who move too slowly for me. I expect them to be able to produce at least a portion of what I can or at least stay out of my way till I achieve.

It takes people like me a long time to learn that not everyone has the same goal or the same drive that I have to achieve. Maybe they are not supposed to. Maybe God gave *me* the vision, or maybe I have, at times, stepped out in my own strength or my own timing. It is much healthier when we learn to move at God's pace. Not too fast, but certainly not too slow. Neither extreme is a good scenario.

My husband, on the other hand, has a real laid back personality. He will probably never have to worry about getting an ulcer. He accepts life as it comes and doesn't set too many high goals. Whatever gets done in a day's time is acceptable to him. The dirty dishes can sit overnight; the house doesn't have to be immaculate to please him. Good news for me, he doesn't have high expectations of me either.

He is a wonderful helpmate. He loves to cook, and grocery shopping is never something that I have to worry about if I don't have the time to do it. He is fantastic at spending time with the kids and taking them with him on errands.

Some time ago, we attended a marriage seminar. The weekend began with a lesson on the different characteristics of a man and a woman. When given time to share, I remarked, "I have a few concerns; the male traits described me to a tee." "Which one?" asked the speaker. He was in shock as I replied, "All of them."

I guess God puts opposites together to balance us out, and we must learn to appreciate each other's differences. I've learned to change the way I look at things. My husband's laid back personality has become a blessing to my head-strong, goal-driven, matter of life and death personality.

Speaking of patience, one day when I was still working outside of my home, I was in the lunch room with several girls. One girl stated that she was looking forward to getting out of there so she could go swimming in her pool. I heard some giggles as I announced, "I don't have a swimming pool. I don't have the patience to care for one." A few minutes went by, and another girl said, "Well, I have to go home and bathe the dog." The laughter turned to a loud roar when I went on to say, "I don't have the patience for dog care either." As the manager giggled uncontrollably, she asked, "Well, Joy, do you have patience with your kids?" I said, "Not always, and since you've asked, be it known I don't do gardens, plants, landscaping, canning or jigsaw puzzles either!"

This patience stuff is taking me a long time to learn. I'm glad God has more patience with me than what I do. As for God's timing, it is usually different than man's timing, especially for people like myself. He's an on-time God!

But... God, Where?

Where did you say you want me to go, Lord? Me, to Latin America? Me, with the prison ministry? Me, to the nursing home? Me, be a Sunday school teacher? Are you sure, Lord? Me, a preacher? I can't see that!

I know a lot of people who are serving in positions that they said they would never serve in. Never say never! These people usually end up very fulfilled in their obedience to the Lord. They are happier than they ever thought that they could be.

More often than not though, I believe the Lord doesn't throw too many surprises on us. At least, not on people like me! He usually uses us where we are at. He causes us to bloom where we are planted. If He is now calling us to an area that we would normally not be comfortable, He prepares us for it. He plants a desire in our heart long before He places us on the battlefield. He puts us through a training course first, as every ministry brings with it some struggles along the way. What He puts on our heart to do, He gives us the resources and the strength to be able to attain it.

You often have to wonder when you see a couple where one of them feels called to do something for the Lord, but the other is dead set against it. I believe that if the Lord leads you to do something, He'll also prepare your spouse.

So where does the problem come in? Maybe the spouse isn't in tune to the voice of God. Maybe he or she isn't at the same level spiritually as the spouse. Maybe he is jealous of the time God will require of her, or of the other people who will get his spouse's attention. But maybe, just maybe, the spouse didn't really hear from God to begin with. Maybe, she is trying to step out in her own strength.

It is so important for a husband/wife relationship to be in unity as to their beliefs, their denomination and their pace of growing in the Lord. There are a lot of struggles in a marriage when a couple is not in agreement in their faith and religious issues.

But God...

But God, who is rich in His greatness and mercy, pours out His love to His children over and over again. He is a great God!

The devil may try to beat you up emotionally, spiritually and physically, *But God* is sufficient! He will see you through.

He gives of Himself to us in a remarkable way. It's fascinating to watch Him move in our lives, on our behalf.

There are so many times I fall short, But God...
There are so many times I am impatient, But God...
There are so many times I get angry, But God...
There are so many times I grow weary, But God...
There are so many times I am anxious, But God...
There are so many times I've been hurt, But God...
There are so many times I get lonely, But God...
There are so many times I am stubborn, But God...
But God... is still awesome, loving, merciful, magnificent, glorious and powerful. But God... is still **God**.

He is the giver of life and life abundant. He will see you through. He cares for His children. He is all-knowing and deals with us with gentleness. His goodness is high above the earth.

He has the bigger picture of your life. He knows what is best. He can see the end result, where we as humans see only what is before us. We walk by sight. He wants to teach us to walk by faith. He watches out for His own as we put our trust in Him.

God's thoughts and ways are greater than man's. He knows why you didn't get that job you wanted; He knows why you had an unplanned pregnancy. He knows why you were running five minutes late.

Not long ago, I had to pick up my middle child from a birthday party one night. As the evening was one of those busy ones, I kept trying to get out the door, but in the process received two phone calls. One was business; the other was a friend who just wanted to talk. I politely had to tell the friend after a while that I had errands to do, including picking up my daughter. Nevertheless, I was running five or ten minutes late as usual. As I was

going up the highway, I was approaching where I needed to turn to get to the birthday party. I noticed the traf-
fic was getting backed up and sirens were flying by.
Looking about 10 to 12 vehicles ahead of me, it was
obvious that there had been a serious accident at the
intersection ahead.

As it turned out, there had been a fatal accident
about five to ten minutes earlier, taking the lives of two
young family members. The vehicle was as flat as a
pancake, nearly impossible for anyone to have lived
through. God had truly spared my life and that of my
youngest child.

A year earlier, we were headed out the door for
Wednesday evening Bible study. I had had an appointment after work that day at a doctor's office that ran
more than an hour late. This put us in a rush, still having to pick up my son and his friend for church. As we
were running out the door, I told my husband, "You go
ahead and take your own car to church. I will go after
the boys."

Our youngest child normally would have ridden
with him, but since they were already in my car, he just
went on. With her being a daddy's girl, I opened my
mouth to call, "Hey, wait for Amanda," and the Holy
Spirit literally shut my mouth. Little did I know when I
was about a third of a mile down the road that my husband was about a third of a mile northbound, wrecking
at a sharp curve in the road into a pole.

On my way to church, I passed a medic unit that
seemed to be in a big hurry. I said a short prayer as I
always do when I see emergency personnel. Little did I
know it was going the wrong way looking for my own

husband. When I got to church, I was met in the parking lot by somebody who had already received the news. I was told that he had simply cut his head and needed some stitches.

As I left the girls at church to go to their classes and took my son with me, it was devastating to drive that last mile to the scene of the accident and see our rural road filled with spectators and ambulances and emergency units everywhere. It was obvious that there was more to it than a cut on the head. My neighbor met me before I got to my husband's car and said, "There's been a change in plans; he's not being taken to the emergency room. They decided to go straight to the Shock Trauma Unit at another hospital." I was numb as I drove home to pick up some extra clothes for him and then straight to the hospital. The day I feared the most was here.

My son and I entered the room where my husband was lying to find blood running into his eyes from his forehead. He had hit the windshield with such great impact that he left a bubble the entire size of his head in the glass. The steering wheel was bent from the grip of his strong arms grasping it to keep him from going through the windshield. All tests came back negative and his life was spared with only a small fracture near the elbow and a skin graft on his forehead. It took days to get all of the glass out of his head.

This was the second time my youngest daughter's safety was protected from a possible accident, as she went with Daddy 99 percent of the time. She was also in a minor car accident at three days old. The Lord has kept His hand on her life.

10

Fingerprints in Time

"But the very hairs of your head are all numbered" (Matthew 10:30).

ingerprints... a unique mark of our identity. It's so hard to comprehend that all of the millions upon millions of fingerprints are so totally different. All of us are made so special and unique by the creator and designer of life. Our all-knowing God created all in His image. He knows all about every one of us. He made all creatures great and small.

Even the hairs on our head are numbered. No two people are alike; all have been given their own unique personality, talents and looks. Some are great achievers; others have more laid-back and easygoing personalities. All are so needed to make up the Body of Christ, the Church.

What's in Your Hand?

Some people have many talents; others have few. But, God only asks that we use what we have in our hands to use. To whom much is given, much is expected. It's usually better to do a few things well than to try to do it all. Over-commitment comes with a high price tag. It shows up in fatigue, moodiness, anger and lack of faithfulness to things we were once fully committed to.

By this stage of my life, I've seen a lot of fantastic people with great zeal for the Lord fall flat on their face from trying to do it all. One of those people is myself! I can't count on both hands how many times I've reached total burnout from trying to be the jack of all trades. Then, I become no good for anything, until I have a few days to recuperate.

So many Christians with good intentions try to be a god to other people. They have a love for people and want to mend their hurting hearts but soon find others are leaning on them like a crutch, and a co-dependent relationship is established. It is easier for the weaker man to pull the stronger man down, than for the stronger man to pull up the pessimistic man.

It is better to point the hurting friend to the Word of God and teach him how to build up his faith in the Lord Jesus Christ and develop a personal relationship with Him. You can share a personal testimonial with him of how the Lord brought you through a similar situation. If you've noticed something that he has done to cause his own problem, you might want to say, "You know one thing I've noticed..." and gently turn the remark into a positive one, encouraging him that you once had some struggles too but this is how you've learned to overcome.

You should offer to pray for the person. I have a high respect for people who stop right then and there during the phone call and ask, "Can I pray with you?" rather than just making the general comment, "Well, I'll keep you in my prayers." It is so much more meaningful if they offer to pray with you right then and there, so that you feel the warmth of their care and become assured that they won't forget.

I went through pure exhaustion too many times before I finally learned that I can't be a god to others who are hurting, even if I've been in their shoes. I can only share personal experience with them, offer them prayer and point them to the cross. They need to get the victory for themselves. We cannot do it for each other.

What's in your hands? Where did God place you? It doesn't matter if you're a manager of a major company or a janitor. He wants you to be the very best servant you can be. Let your light shine in your corner of the earth.

Personally, I am a medical transcriber. I used to get overwhelmed typing the office notes on all of the doctor's visits and hearing nothing but problems and illnesses all day long. Now, I have learned to use this valuable time to minister to the needs of others by the art of intercession.

What an opportunity to intercede on the behalf of others who may not have anyone else praying for them. They come into the doctor's office with anything from common illnesses to terminal diseases, mental problems, AIDs and those suffering tragedies in their lives. As I type the notes on their visit to the doctor, I have learned to touch the throne of God on their behalf. We'll never know until we get to Glory how far our prayers go.

What Marks Are You Leaving in Life?

We all have left marks of some type from things that we were involved in. There are tire marks just a third of a mile up the road from our home that remind me of how the Lord spared my husband's life in his car accident. My enlarged left pupil reminds me of what unequal pupil dilation could have been the result of. The birthmark on the back of my one leg is a reminder that many people are born with very serious birth defects. Many people have scars, be it in body, soul or spirit, that remind them of the pain of their past.

The marks we leave on earth will tell the next generation a lot about us. We need to consider carefully what we will be remembered for when we pass from this life into eternity.

Have you ever completed a project you've been working on and thought, "Wow, what an influence will this have on others? This is a unique creation. What kind of mark will it leave in this life?" Or did you ever leave yourself a note to remind yourself to do something and wonder who would find these thoughts you just jotted down if you fall over dead today? What will they think? Will they understand what this meant?

Are the marks that you are leaving good or bad? If you pass away as a result of a heart attack, what will your family members find when they go through your personal belongings? Will they be proud? Will they be devastated? Will they be shocked by the hidden things you were involved in? What will they think of your diary? Should you resign your job today or leave this old world, what will you be remembered for? Your hard work... your laziness? Your smile? Your frown? Your kindness? Your harshness? Your uplifting words? Your gossip? Your reliability? Your tardiness? Your accuracy? Your sloppiness? Your love? Your bitterness?

When the minister is called upon to preach for your funeral, will it be difficult for him to tell good stories in remembrance of your life? Or will he have to sugar coat a few things? Will he be able to say, "Beyond a doubt, I know that your dear family member made heaven his home?" or will he have to use the general words "eternal destiny"? Will your vacancy in this life be missed, or have you lived a fruitless life?

Given the chance, what would you pick to have inscribed on your tombstone? "See ya soon!" "Glory Bound." "Going Home." "It's been good to know ya." I once saw a tombstone that said, "This one's on me." How interesting!

What will your loved ones be able to say about you if they write a poem to be read at your funeral? Have you made a good mark in life?

Will your church leaders struggle to fill your shoes, or were you just a spectator? Were you actively involved in the lives of others, or did you warm a pew each Sunday morning?

What imprint have you left on the lives of your children? Have you taught them kindness, faith and love? Do you show them the importance of humbleness? Of patience? Does joy fill your home, even when life gets chaotic? Is there peace and trust in God during the storms of life?

Do your children witness some of your devotional time with the Lord? Do you pray as a family? Can they share their hurting hearts with you in moments of a need for comfort?

Are manners and grace for the meal practiced at the dinner table? Are good personal habits and cleanliness taking place? Is there respect for each other's feelings, privacy and belongings?

Is your body the temple of God? Do you abuse it via use of tobacco, drugs, alcohol, caffeine or excessive eating habits? Do you groom yourself reasonably well? How about the importance of physical exercise, vitamins and good eating habits?

Do you talk well of others, yourself and your family? Does your family hear you voice thanks for God's goodness in your life? Do you listen to wholesome music which brings glory to the Lord? What comes across the radio station, the television set? What about the affects of the video games and computer programs your kids are exposed to?

What comes out of your mouth? Encouragement, kindness? Acceptance of each other's personality differences, likes and dislikes?

What is on the inside *will* come out one way or another. If you squeeze a lemon, orange juice doesn't come out. During times of stress in our lives, we find out what is on the inside. Oh, the shock we experience sometimes when it comes pouring out!

We go through life trying to wear a mask. God delights in our honesty. We can't hide our feelings from God. He knows what is going on inside, and it is going to come out one way or another. It's time we throw away our masks, leave behind the crutches we lean on and develop a spiritual backbone.

When you leave this old world, what treasures will you leave behind? Some beautiful artwork? An original poem? A manuscript to an article you were writing? Memories of love and kind deeds?

Will there be treasures stored in a large bank account or treasures in the heavenlies? Will there be the evidence of poverty? Of great debt? What will your family members pull out of your closet?

Will you hear the words, "Well done thou good and faithful servant, enter into the joy of the Lord?" Or will the devastation of, "Depart from Me, ye worker of iniquity, I never knew you," haunt you eternally?

What marks will you leave in the book of your life?

Vanity

Do you realize how much time we as Christians waste? I'm convinced it's one of Satan's most effective tools. Stop and think about it. He doesn't come into our lives with a big bang. He subtly sneaks into the little cracks in our lives. It comes in the form of over busyness. It comes in the form of having our focus on the petty things of life, our little aches and pains and complaints.

We seem to usually have the inability to just shake things off. We dwell on them and thus magnify the problem. I've been guilty many times. If I would have only said, "God Bless You," and walked away.

I've watch this horrible scenario destroy whole church bodies as its members spend most of their time warring against each other. Always having eyes on the specks of another's faults and failing to pull out their own beam.

We twentieth century Christians seem to have our focus on the business, the administration of our church groups, rather than on the ministry. The devil has a hay day watching us run in circles. No strength, no vision.

All of the time we spend complaining, gossiping, repenting and cleaning up our messes could be used in valuable time witnessing, interceding and worshiping our Creator! Wow, what a powerful impact we would have on the world if every time we are tempted to complain about another person and cut them down, we stop and intercede for God's divine intervention!

I once worked in an office with a group of a half a dozen ladies. The supervisor spent a lot of time in the manager's office. She wasn't a happy camper. When she was at her desk, the typical conversation in the room was that of numerous complaints. She felt that the work load in our department was immense.

Hour after hour, day after day, week after week, month after month, I listened to the same old woes. It put knots in my stomach, being a very inward, shy person at that time in my life.

Finally, one day when she stormed out the door to the manager's office, I had had enough. I jumped up from my desk and blurted out, "If that lady would spend half of the time working that she spends complaining, we would get our responsibilities done in 40 hours a week, and she would find she has no grounds to stand on!"

Remind you of anybody? Unfortunately, it reminds me of the Church. We spend so much time trying to work out all of the technicalities, planning and arranging of things to suit ourselves, complaining, bickering and wailing, that we forget what we have been called to do.

I once had a friend who, every time we visited with each other, told me how badly the churches today have gone downhill. They have failed to minister to a certain age group of people who are dear to her heart. After a number of months, I finally realized my friend had it all wrong. She had to stop wasting time complaining and start exerting that energy into fulfilling the vision that the Lord had laid on *her* heart to do for that age group.

Are you wasting precious time? Has the Lord laid something on your heart? Are you making excuses and procrastinating? Are you passing the buck, trying to say that God called your pastor to do it? Ministers can't do it all. They are only human; they have only as much time and energy as we do. God needs to use lay people in the Church more than ever. The time is so short.

What talent have you been holding back on? The Lord takes your best and does great things with it. He will use you where you are at. Remember, He doesn't expect from you what He doesn't provide the grace and strength to fulfill.

— 11 —
Is There Such a Thing?

*"So then because thou art lukewarm, and nei-
ther cold nor hot, I will spew thee out of my
mouth"* (Revelation 3:16).

So is there such a thing? Such a thing as what?? Is there such a thing as just enough of heaven to keep you out of hell?

The Lord Himself says in Revelation that He will spew the lukewarm out of His mouth! This clearly indicates that there really is not such a thing as the familiar statement we use, "just enough heaven to keep us out of hell." Christ is coming for a church without spot or wrinkle. He wants us to be sold out to Him. We need to be on fire for the cause of the Gospel.

Life Abundant

Be assured my friend, it is a delight to serve the Lord. The longer I serve Him, the sweeter He grows; it's a reality in the lives of countless, born-again believers.

"I am come that they might have life, and that they might have *it* more abundantly" (John 10:10).

Great news! Not only did Jesus die for us to give us life when we were dead in our sins, but He gives in plenty the riches of life. The Christian walk should not be burdensome. We can take great pleasure in serving Him and living uprightly.

"O the depth of the riches both of the wisdom and knowledge of God! How unsearchable are his judgments, and his ways past finding out!" (Romans 11:33).

Grasp the Eternal Picture

"If ye then be risen with Christ, seek those things which are above, where Christ sitteth on the right hand of God. Set your affection on things above, not on things on the earth. For ye are dead, and your life is hid with Christ in God. When Christ, who is our life, shall appear, then shall ye also appear with him in glory" (Colossians 3:1-4).

This is my favorite New Testament passage of Scripture. It speaks of treasures in the heavenlies. It strengthens me to strive for the things of eternal value. It encourages me to keep on trucking for the Lord.

"Ye doubtless, and I count all things but loss for the excellency of the knowledge of Christ Jesus my Lord: For whom I have suffered the loss of all things, and do count them but dung, that I may win Christ" (Philippians 3:8).

Are you carrying baggage that will crumble to naught when the trumpet sounds? Are you spending your time in vain? Are you easily upset about something that is petty in comparison to the glory that we shall receive someday? In light of eternity, what will it matter?

We tend to dwell on the good ole days. We live in our past. We must remember that that was then, and this is now. That blessing that we once had in our lives may no longer be there, but does it matter?

Fifteen years into my marriage, I found myself 50 pounds heavier than I was on my wedding day. I decided to go on a diet, hoping to lose 20 to 30 pounds. Once I lost the weight, was I still 25 pounds overweight? No! I had been 25 pounds underweight when I got married.

We always tend to reflect on the past. We get so set in our ways that we don't want to change. Sometimes we want so badly to bring back the good ole days that we forget that the good ole days really weren't so good after all. They were our childhood days when we were drinking from the bottle. Just precious memories. We've grown up now, and God is moving us on to bigger and better things.

In light of eternity, what does it matter if we are a few pounds overweight? What does it matter if we never got to go on that vacation that we always wanted to go on? What does it matter if we got our feelings hurt?

Let's remember the things that we've learned in the previous chapters that will count in eternity. Are we sure we are saved? How many others are we witnessing to? Are we spending adequate time with our family? Serving in the Church? Meditating on the Word?

"For the Lord himself shall descend from heaven with a shout, with the voice of the archangel, and with the trump of God: and the dead in Christ shall rise first: Then we which are alive and remain shall be caught up together with them in the clouds, to meet the Lord in the air: and so shall we ever be with the Lord" (I Thessalonians 4:16,17).

Are you sure that you're sure that you're sure that you'll be included in the rapture of the Saints? Are you looking for His appearance?

Many times, people comment what the first thing is that they plan on doing when they get to heaven. It's funny to listen to some of the things they can't wait to do. "I am going to take a nice long vacation." "Well, I am going to go looking for my grandma." "I am going to have a mansion on a hillside." "I am going to ask God why I had to suffer so." "I am going to ask the Apostle Paul how he did it all." The list goes on and on.

I have my doubts if any of these people will get their wish. I have an inkling that as soon as we enter those pearly gates, every one of us is going to fall at the feet of Jesus and say, "What have I ever done to deserve such grace?" All of the cares of this old world will crumble at His appearing. We will stand in awe of His majesty.

Keep pressing on my friend. It will be worth it all when we see His face.

"I press toward the mark for the prize of the high calling of God in Christ Jesus" (Philippians 3:14).

— 12 —
The Blooood!!

"...But ye are washed, but ye are sanctified, but ye are justified in the name of the Lord Jesus, and by the Spirit of our God" (Corinthians 6:11).

Some time ago, I was listening to a Christian radio broadcast. The interviewer asked, "What does it mean to be saved?" There was a large range of answers given from different ages and all walks of life, such as, "doing good," "going to church," reading the Bible," "living right," "praying." I stopped dead in my trail and shouted loudly, "To be blooood washed!!!"

I've been a Christian most of my life, yet apart from the blood of Jesus Christ, I am nothing. I cannot do it on my own! "I am crucified with Christ: nevertheless I live; yet not I, but Christ liveth in me: and the life which I now live in the flesh I live by the faith of the Son of God, who loved me, and gave himself for me" (Galatians 2:20).

We need to realize that *everyone* needs to have a salvation experience for himself. We tend to think that the drug addict and the rapist are the ones who really need to find the Lord, but what about the sweet little old lady down the street who will bend over backwards to do anything for you? She may have a heart of gold, but unless she has accepted the Lord as her personal Savior, she is in as much danger of judgment as the "real bad sinner." In the eyes of God, one sin is as deadly as another, no matter how great or small.

I recently attended my first "Awake America" Crusade by the Brownsville Revival Team. The services were fantastic. The worship was great, along with the preaching of the Word, the excitement, the fellowship and the mini vacation. Nothing, however, compared to some comments that were made at the end of the altar call about the blood of Jesus. It's our only way to the cross. All of the praises, jumping up and down, frills and thrills and outstanding music did not begin to compare to my appreciation for the Blood!

Afterwards, this appreciation for the Blood became a deeper reality as I went with a group from our church out for a late night meal. Dozens of people were at the restaurant who had just come from the crusade. In fact, we ate at this particular restaurant two nights in a row.

Everyone's attention was drawn to three young people who came in dressed for some attention. Some had spiked hair. Some had green hair, and their clothes were obviously not that of a Christian. One boy stood out most of all. He was dressed to imitate Jesus. He wore a white robe with a crown of thorns and a very spiked hairdo. Mixed feelings were great among those who had just come from services where they had experienced a great Move of God. The young boy was obviously mocking our Lord and Savior. When confronted by one bold Christian girl, he proudly claimed that he didn't need her prayers, in fact he wrote the Book. Some people were outraged at his disrespect for Christianity, and others responded in feelings of fear.

All of us were greatly moved and humbled as one of the guys from our church group made a great impression on the three young people and on our entire church. About ten minutes after being seated at our booths, he quietly got up and walked clear across the restaurant to the other side where the three nonbelievers sat. A minute later, he returned. The place grew quiet as we all wondered what in the world he had been up to. Being a very quiet gentleman, his move surprised us greatly.

He came back, sat down at his table and soon started shaking and crying. He got up and left the restaurant for a few minutes. His wife explained to us that the Lord had convicted him to go over to their table and say a few kind words, and he simply could not get comfortable until he did. We were all moved by his act of compassion as she told us he simply said to the three nonbelievers, "You know, you may look a lot different than me and act different than me, but you are God's creation just like I am. The only difference between yourselves and myself is the fact that I have been saved by the blood of Jesus." The Blooood!!! The difference!

Soon the gentleman from our church returned. We were all moved as we watched him radiate with the power of God like we had never seen him before. God was doing a supernatural work in his life, and it all began with a simple act of obedience and compassion.

As we watched, we commented what a great thing had just taken place before our eyes and, of all places, in the middle of the night in a restaurant! At that, several of us burst out as the spirit of laughter came all over us. It began with one table and spread to the two other tables that were with our church.

Within a few minutes, we heard a man about six tables down break into a loud uncontrollable laughter. He had just come from the revival services also. Some of the people at his table were lying across their chairs and falling on the floor from laughing uncontrollably. It didn't last for just a minute or two. It went on for quite some time!

The manager came out and stood by the salad bar in total confusion at what had broken out in his restaurant. Some were laying on the floor; others were spread across a booth as the joy of the Lord swept through each of our tables.

I had totally forgotten about the three people that were sitting at the other end, obviously in great need of salvation. Before I knew it, the young girl with green hair went flying by and into the restroom area. Oh boy, I thought, I bet she's upset. Her spirit is going to be outraged at the light she sees shining through us.

A couple of girls went to check on her. Believe it or not, she had been so overcome with laughter herself that she literally got sick to her stomach! God was doing a work in her life. She and her two friends had come into the restaurant, knowing that over 12,000 people had just come out of a great revival service in their town. They had come to draw attention to themselves and to let it be known that they did not believe in God.

What the enemy had meant for evil, God used for His glory. As we departed to our motel rooms that night, we all gathered in prayer to agree that these three nonbelievers would soon come to the saving knowledge of Jesus Christ.

People are constantly running to and fro searching for peace and happiness where peace can't be found. It was already provided for 2000 years ago when Christ died upon the cross for each and every one of us. The answer will never be found in the things that this old world has to offer. No millionaire on the earth can buy you the happiness and joy that comes through the precious blood of Jesus. Stop searching for the answer, dear friend. He has already made a way.

"Forasmuch as ye know that ye were not redeemed with corruptible things, as silver and gold, from your vain conversation received by tradition from your fathers; But with the precious blood of Christ, as of a lamb without blemish and without spot" (I Peter 1:18,19).

It's the Blood that covers me when I fall short. It's the Blood that covers me when I am slow to hear, quick to speak and even when I blow my stack. It's the Blood that covers me when my mind wanders to places it shouldn't. There's not one of us that can attain salvation on his own. We've all sinned; there is none righteous, no not one! "If thou, Lord, shouldest mark iniquities, O Lord, who shall stand?" (Psalm 130:3). We must never be so foolish as to think that we have arrived! The more we commit to God and clean up in our lives, the more we seem to find. It's kind of like cleaning closets – an ongoing job.

We continuously need to fill our spiritual gas tanks up. It only lasts so long; then we need to refuel. Just like we have to bathe ourselves daily and clean our physical bodies on an ongoing basis, we need to wash up spiritually for that fresh new cleansing on the inside.

"By the grace of God I am what I am" (I Corinthians 15:10).

Now we can't go about doing our own thing because of this grace. "What shall we say then? Shall we continue in sin, that grace may abound? God forbid. How shall we, that are dead to sin, live any longer therein?" (Romans 6:1,2). We cannot tempt God and see how much we can get away with. We are expected to continuously be trying to walk in the Will of God, always trying to get closer to Him through the reading of the Word and prayer. Everyday we need to eat, give our bodies new nourishment. The same is true of our spiritual lives.

I get so sick of hearing well meaning titles on how to get God's attention. You know, *How to Get a Financial Blessing*, *Ten Steps to Having Your Prayers Answered*, *The Best Way to Study the Bible*, *How to Get Your Spouse Saved*. It's made to sound like there's a magic button we have to find to reach God.

It's like a fairy tale! Just press the red button, then the blue button, take three steps to the right, one giant step forward, and then an angel will meet you and ask, "Is it behind curtain number one, curtain number two or curtain number three?" If you select the correct curtain, you will have picked the magic formula to touching the heart of God and live happily ever after!

We used to hear so much about God's free salvation. Now it seems all we hear is, "Now that you're a Christian, you have to do this and that." Read three chapters of the Bible a day, pray one hour everyday, support your local church and missions, give all you have to the poor, and don't forget the television evangelist. Serve on three committees in your church, teach Sunday school, begin a women's Bible study, visit the nursing home, prisons, children's homes. Prepare a meal once a week to entertain guests in your home – that is, your spotless home, the one where you home-school all four of your exceptionally well-mannered children who wear only homemade clothing, eat three well-balanced, home-cooked meals a day, and certainly never get caught with curlers in your hair!

We spend so much of our time listening to what Mr. Right is telling us God's Will is for our lives. We are infatuated with what Mr. Evangel says God's Word for the Church is today.

Seek God, my Christian friend, and He will establish your steps. He will walk with you and talk with you. He will love you just as you are and meet you at your point of need. As you continue to grow in Him and seek first the Kingdom of God, all of these other things will come in order. The closer we get to God, the more we'll want to do those good Christian deeds. If we learn how to hear His voice – not our neighbor's, our friend's or even our pastor's – we will know what He has called us as individuals to do. We can't do it all. That's the unique purpose of the Body of Christ, each member in its place.

The Alpha and Omega

If our life is truly in His hand, does it matter when He moves in a different way than we expected Him to? I had to go through years of "hell and high water" in order for the Lord to teach me He is in control.

I've always been a worrisome person, always analyzing everything, trying to keep everything under control at all times. God forbid that Joy should ever lose it. But... God! in His rich mercy took me to rock bottom, allowing one trial after another to enter my life until all of the resources I had leaned on were pulled out from under me. I lost my cool many times before I finally learned to turn all controls over to Him. The battle was the Lord's!

A lot of people go through life trying to leave their mark, their handiwork, their talents, abilities and performance. But, He is undoubtedly the Alpha and Omega, the beginning and the end. Stop searching every corner of the earth trying to find the answer. We already have it. Rest in the Great I Am!

We sometimes put ourselves through many hard-core lessons, be it in need for salvation, deliverance, provision or healing, only to learn in the ultimate end that He is still the answer. He's been waiting all along for us to move from the driver's seat over to the passenger's seat. Hand Him the steering wheel and relax in His divine wisdom. Give Him the controls. What is over our head is under His feet!

I encourage you, my friend, to sow your treasures up in heavenly places with Jesus Christ. It's the only lasting treasure you will find.

"And he said unto me, It is done. I am Alpha and Omega, the beginning and the end. I will give unto him that is athirst of the fountain of the water of life freely" (Revelation 21:6).